UNCONVENTIONAL INVESTING

Alternative Strategies Beyond Just Stocks & Bonds and Buy & Hold

Tim Higgins, CFP(r), ChFC(r) & Michael Hajek III, CPA

Copyright © 2014 Tim Higgins, CFP(r), ChFC(r) & Michael Hajek III, CPA
All rights reserved.

ISBN: 1492105953
ISBN 13: 9781492105954

You need a game plan, but you can do better than the traditional balanced portfolio of 60 percent stocks and 40 percent bonds.

www.unconventional-investing.com

Limit of Liability/Disclaimer of Warranty: While the authors have used their best efforts in preparing this book, they make no representations or warranties with respect to the accuracy or completeness of the contents of this book and specifically disclaim any implied warranties of merchantability or fitness for a particular purpose. The advice and strategies contained herein may not be suitable for your situation. You should consult with a professional where appropriate. Neither author shall be liable for any loss of profit or any other commercial damages, including but not limited to special, incidental, consequential, or other damages.

CHAPTERS

Introduction ·vii
Chapter 1   Questioning the Conventional Wisdom of the Classic Sixty–
              Forty Portfolio · 1
Four Major Headwinds to the Average Investor's Success · · · · · · · · · · · · · 11
Chapter 2   Behavioral Psychology: You Are Your Own Worst Enemy · · · · 13
Chapter 3   Common Misconceptions about Conventional Investing · · · · · 31
Chapter 4   Where Are We and Where Are We Going? · · · · · · · · · · · · · · 61
Chapter 5   Stocks, Bonds, Cash, and the Tragic 401(K) Handcuff · · · · · · · 87
Five Unconventional Solutions · 99
Chapter 6   Specific Asset-Class Solutions to Inflation and Rising Rates · · 101
Chapter 7   Alternative Investing · 117
Chapter 8   Tactical Asset Allocation · 155
Chapter 9   Trend Analysis: Winning by Not Losing · · · · · · · · · · · · · · · 181
Chapter 10 Self-Directed Retirement Accounts · · · · · · · · · · · · · · · · · · · 221
Chapter 11 Tax-Efficient Investing for Your Retirement and
               College Goals · 241

Note:
Chapters four, five, six, eight, and nine solely contain the
information and opinions of Tim Higgins.
Chapter ten solely contains the information and opinions of Mike Hajek.

INTRODUCTION

Within the following pages you will hear from a Certified Financial Planner™ practitioner and a certified public accountant on an assortment of financial strategies. What motivated us to write this book stemmed from our shared frustration with what passes as conventional financial wisdom. We find that this advice is typically un-tailored, outdated, less efficient, and not what many on Main Street (the common investor) truly desires. Therefore, our goal with this book is to provide a resource to any investor that is willing to step outside-the-box and consider some different ideas and insights. Giving consideration to these concepts will be like trying a specific food for the first time. You might like it or hate it, but it still provides valuable feedback for future dining. Helping you accept or reject specific strategies will help solidify your conviction with the game plan you ultimately choose, and that is valuable.

We see financial solutions moving in the direction of automated investment strategies. These types of solutions remove decision making from the investor (e.g., target date retirement funds). In an attempt to prevent individuals from hurting themselves by getting too hands-on, the industry is apparently encouraging simple solutions as if it is the be-all and end-all. There is a time and a place for such strategies, but we feel that this is not that time. Not only are we encouraging different ways to think and examine your own planning, we are also encouraging personal responsibility and proactiveness. We feel this is the best way to protect oneself. We feel that being an educated, informed, proactive manager of your own finances could pay large dividends moving forward.

Our disclaimer is that these are our opinions. We arrived at these opinions through our own research, and we believe they hold weight. Are you entitled to disagree with us? Absolutely. That is your right. We applaud the fact that you entertain new points of view. However, you might agree with us that, for example, buying and holding a portfolio of 60 percent stocks and 40 percent bonds forever is not the best strategy moving forward. If so, then you will know that you are part of a growing group of critical thinkers who feel that in these uncommon times we need uncommon, out-of-the-box solutions to stay one step ahead. Outsourcing your financial future to a target date retirement fund at first glance may sound like a tailored strategy, but if it doesn't adapt to the current environment it is in, how effective can it be? In today's world we know we need to do better. The authors don't implement such strategies, and in the following pages you will learn why.

Lastly, the title of this book comes from its primary theme. We think it is important for individuals to take a step back from groupthink. **Herd mentality is typically based on old information.** In a world in which information is moving faster than ever, you need new and better ideas to stay ahead. Implementing old ideas usually leaves you lagging, and that may negatively affect your chances of achieving what really matters: owning a home, educating your children, and being able to live comfortably in your golden years. What worked twenty years ago doesn't necessarily work today, and what works today might not work in twenty years. As the great hockey player Wayne Gretzky once said, "I skate to where the puck is going to be, not where it has been." Either way, you are either accomplishing what you want to accomplish or you aren't.

In chapter one we will analyze and question the conventional wisdom of buying and holding the classic balanced (sixty–forty) portfolio. Chapters two through five will outline the major headwinds that investors face when making prudent portfolio decisions. The next six chapters will introduce you to general and specific solutions to help you proactively navigate through those headwinds. Please note that these solutions are not necessarily convenient or easy to implement, as most of them require initiative and personal responsibility. If these requirements do not deter you, we believe you will be better off after exploring, researching, and implementing the ideas in this book. Lastly, everyone's situation is unique. A qualified advisor should help you figure out the specific advice that applies to you, if you feel ill-equipped to handle it on your own.

> **Quick Synopsis**
>
> Conventional wisdom (and most of mainstream media) promote three ideas:
> 1. The two asset classes you need to own are stocks and bonds.
> 2. Own a good balance between the two, preferably 60 percent stocks and 40 percent bonds.
> 3. Buy and hold.
>
> This book will explain why the conventional wisdom is impractical today and why these widely promoted concepts may be less than ideal.

Whom this book is for: We did not write this book for financial professionals; rather it is for everyday people (parents, business owners, retirees, students, etc.). It is our intention to describe our concepts for universal appeal. If these concepts are new to you, we understand that you might have to read certain passages multiple times.

How to read this book: We recommend that you read it from cover to cover. However, you can skip over specific chapters without drastically impacting your comprehension. In addition, rather than providing endless footnotes, we have provided easy-access web links throughout the book.

CHAPTER 1

QUESTIONING THE CONVENTIONAL WISDOM OF THE CLASSIC SIXTY–FORTY PORTFOLIO

Question: Conventional wisdom contends that we should buy and hold a balanced portfolio, but is this the best strategy moving forward?

To quote from John (Jack) Bogle's (the founder of The Vanguard Group) CNBC interview conducted on April 1, 2013, **"Prepare for at least two declines of twenty-five to thirty percent, maybe even fifty percent in the coming decade. Trying to guess when it is going to go way up or way down is simply not a productive way to put your money to work."**

A video of the interview can be found here: http://video.cnbc.com/gallery/?video=3000158038.

Bogle is the pioneer of promoting buy-and-hold, low-cost investing and viewed by many as a true champion for the small investor. Ironically, his forecast and advice for many average investors may seem to go together like oil and water. First, you should expect at least *two* large-scale declines in your portfolio within the next ten years (i.e., more pain is on the way). Second, strap on your seat belt, hold your breath, and be ready to buy and hold through the entire roller coaster ride (i.e., don't do anything about it).

Upon further review, the key to his advice is not to guess at market tops and bottoms, and we wholeheartedly agree that guessing is no way to efficiently manage a portfolio. However, the question we need to ask is are we helpless in the face of such prognostications? Bogle's quote perfectly sums up the purpose behind this book, and we are here to share some solutions for your consideration.

We both began our current careers in the nineties, when the consensus view was that buy-and-hold was the best strategy for all investors. Since there is no way to accurately time the market consistently, you might as well purchase a mix of stocks and bonds, and you might as well hold them for the long term. Whenever there is a dip in the markets, don't worry. They will most certainly go back up.

In the late nineties this was the doctrine of the investment community also imparted onto me at the start of my (Tim's) career (June 1999). How has this doctrine served investors throughout since then? As you can see on the following chart, there has been a lot of volatility and only very modest gains. A $100,000 investment in the Vanguard 500 Index Fund fourteen and a half years later would have been worth $168,268. Over that time period, the average annual return was 3.63 percent. I don't think most investors would be thrilled with that return, given the amount of volatility they had to endure.

*Note: Most of that positive annual return attributable to the final two years.

Questioning the Conventional Wisdom of the Classic Sixty–Forty Portfolio

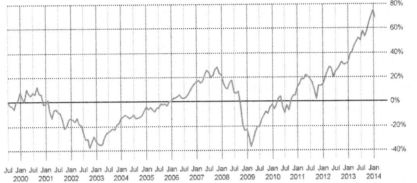

We believe that buy-and-hold is a better strategy than trying to time the market (timing being defined here by guessing when a top or bottom has formed). However, we think you can do better and could have done better than the 3.63 percent annual return over the past 14.5 years. Also, those close to retirement *need* to do better, especially if inflation alone is in the 3 percent range. Here are some atypical ideas to help get you started on better portfolio construction and management. We appreciate everything that Vanguard offers, and we actually recommend some of their strategies in this book. But is that the best we can do as individual investors?

In 2012, *Money* magazine interviewed Andrew Lo, an economist and finance professor at MIT's Sloan School of Management. He echoed some thoughts that are very much in line with the premise of this book. We wish to share these thoughts with the average investor. Here is a portion of his interview:

"**Lo:** Buy-and-hold doesn't work anymore. The volatility is too significant. Almost any asset can suddenly become much more risky. Buying into a mutual fund and holding it for 10 years is no longer going to deliver the same kind of expected return that we saw over the course of the last seven decades, simply because of the nature of financial markets and how complex it's gotten.

***Money* magazine:** Okay, but even during the so-called lost decade (2000 to 2010) someone who regularly put money into a 60% stock/40% bond portfolio would have had about a 4% return. Why isn't that good enough?

Lo: Think about how the person earned 4%. He lost 30%, saw a big bounce-back, and so on, and the compound rate of return over the period was 4%. But most investors did not wait for the dust to settle. After the first 25% loss, they probably reduced their holdings, and only got part way back in after the market somewhat recovered.

Lo: It's human behavior. Ask actual investors what their net rate of return was over the last three years, and see if it's the same rate returned by the market. I bet you it's not.

***Money* magazine:** So what choice do I have instead?

Lo: We're in an awkward period of our industry where we haven't developed good alternatives. Your best bet is to hold a variety of mutual funds that have relatively low fees and try to manage the volatility within a reasonable range. You should be diversified not just with stocks and bonds but also across the entire spectrum of investment opportunities: stocks, bonds, currencies, commodities, and domestically and internationally.

Lo: Most of us didn't sign up for the kind of volatility we're seeing right now. So keep in mind that if you're holding equities, you are probably taking more risk than you thought."

There are three points to stress from this excerpt:

1. Volatility has been amplified whether you signed up for large market fluctuations or not. This is the new environment with online accounts and high-frequency trading. We need to adapt to this.

2. Volatility and human emotions do not mix well. We will discuss how people need to have systems or game plans to help harness their emotions. Emotions don't help you invest.
3. Beyond stocks and bonds, we need to be exposed to new and different asset classes. We categorize these asset classes as alternatives, and we will make the case for why you need to add them to your portfolio.

Brett Arends is a senior columnist for MarketWatch and a personal finance columnist for the *Wall Street Journal*. Like Andrew Lo, Arends critiques this conventional wisdom quite well in his June 2012 article, "If both stocks and bonds are expensive, a 'balanced' portfolio may not work." In the article, Arends points out that there have been long periods of time when a sixty–forty portfolio (60 percent stocks and 40 percent bonds), rebalanced regularly, produced little return after adjusting for inflation. For example, 1927–1931 achieved a -3.2 percent return, 1937–1950 achieved a 0.2 percent return, and 1965–1982 achieved a -0.3 percent return. The article suggests that to give investors reliable returns, a balanced portfolio needs to include more than just stocks and bonds. He concludes by stating, "There is no perfect solution…But investors need to be braced for the possibility that the fund industry's simplistic solutions, as well as its optimistic forecasts, come with absolutely no guarantees."

> Unfortunately, within America's favorite retirement (401(k)s, 403(b)s) and college savings plans (529s) are where we often find simplistic solutions with limited other choices.

But will buy-and-hold and a sixty–forty portfolio work in the future?

The widely accepted efficient market hypothesis argues that if every security is fairly valued at all times, then there is really no point to trade. This may lead us to assume that our best game plan is to purchase our stocks and bonds and never sell them. Simple advice, but is it that easy to implement? Try telling this to people who retired in 1999 or 2007, before the most recent two major bear markets. I wonder whether they think that this is sound advice or potentially harmful advice. Oftentimes what worked well in the past will not work equally as well in the future. Buy-and-hold may have produced excellent results in the bull markets of the eighties and nineties, but since then, it may not have been the most efficient game plan for your hard-earned savings.

A critical element that is not often discussed in the buy-and-hold argument is that the strategy works best if the investor enters the market closer to a bottom than a peak. The argument for buy-and-hold goes against trying to time the market. Ironically, the argument is that you cannot do it. However, buy-and-hold works best if you time the market correctly. For example, imagine an investor lump-summing (i.e., depositing or investing at one time) a large amount of savings into the NASDAQ market in 1999 or into a new home in 2006. He or she may be totally on board with buy-and-hold, but because the timing is poor—something the investor could not have totally foreseen—it will take a long time before these assets appreciate.

As we evaluate the most recent past with an eye toward the future, I encourage you to begin using the logical left side of your brain as well as your intuition on this matter (normally we wouldn't want to do this in the context of investment advice, but for a macro perspective, it helps set up our discussion). Does the economic environment of the past few years feel the same as previous ones, or does it feel different to you?

- What do you think when you hear of massive bailouts of major financial institutions?
- What do you think about the government stepping in to save General Motors, the country's largest car manufacturer?

- What do you think about the flash crash in 2010, in which the Dow Jones Industrial Average dropped approximately one thousand points within minutes?
- What do you think about MF Global, which is now bankrupt, inexplicably losing over $1.2 billion in customer funds?
- What do you think about the idea suggested that the United States should mint a trillion-dollar platinum coin to then deposit at the Fed to give the government enough money to pay its debts?
- *New York Times* columnist Paul Krugman floated the idea that an alien invasion would fix the economy (http://business.time.com/2011/08/16/paul-krugman-an-alien-invasion-could-fix-the-economy/).
- In what seems like a daily occurrence, European countries are in need of additional bailouts to stay afloat. In the case of Cyprus, they needed a "bail in" from the depositors' accounts.
- What do you think about the city of Detroit declaring bankruptcy?
- According to the *Washington Post*, over *forty-seven million people* in the United States now rely on food stamps.

I don't know about you, but this sure doesn't feel normal to me.

We believe that unconventional times call for unconventional measures. We refer to our approach as unconventional because many of our strategies aren't currently mainstream. Perhaps they are less common because they actually promote individual education and proactive management. Most publications shy away from such recommendations because they believe that when individual investors have more control, they increase their chances of hurting themselves. Conversely, when you rely on conventional wisdom and follow the herd, you remain average with regard to what the herd is doing. Interestingly, the media does not consider it hurting yourself if in a major bear market your portfolio is down 30 percent, as long as everyone else's (the herd) is the same.

In our view, losing money hurts whether you do it alone or with a group. We personally don't want to be average. We don't like relying on conventional wisdom and rules of thumb that have proven in recent bear markets to provide little help. To best protect our families and ourselves financially, we need to first educate ourselves. Secondly, we need to honestly evaluate where we currently stand. Thirdly, we desire to be above average. Lastly, we should be proactive and take action. Like a CFO of a company, we should entertain all creative ideas. We should decide on a course of action and implement it.

> Additional articles on diverging from the buy-and-hold mantra:
>
> http://money.cnn.com/2012/03/02/pf/efficient_market.moneymag/index.htm
>
> http://www.kiplinger.com/article/investing/T052-C017-S001-buy-and-hold-is-risky.html
>
> http://www.forbes.com/sites/jakezamansky/2012/07/05/the-death-of-the-buy-and-hold-investor/
>
> http://articles.marketwatch.com/2011-08-01/commentary/30758547_1_stock-market-gdp-economy
>
> http://blogs.wsj.com/totalreturn/2012/11/07/why-buy-and-hold-feels-dead/
>
> http://www.forbes.com/sites/marcprosser/2012/12/14/jeff-gundlach-3-ways-to-profit-from-the-coming-financial-catastrophe/
>
> http://blog.annuitythinktank.com/wp-content/uploads/2012/06/buy-hold-stock-strategy-officially-dead.pdf

> **In summary**
> - Market volatility has been amplified.
> - Volatility and human emotions are a bad mix.
> - Beyond stocks and bonds, we need to investigate new and different asset classes (alternatives).

First, we need to acknowledge the obstacles that we are up against.

For years, the investment industry has tried to scare clients into staying fully invested in the stock market at all times, no matter how high stocks go.... It's hooey.... They're leaving out more than half the story.

—*Wall Street Journal* columnist Brett Arends

FOUR MAJOR HEADWINDS TO THE AVERAGE INVESTOR'S SUCCESS

1. Human Emotions

2. Investment Ignorance

3. Current Economic Environment

4. The Tragic 401(k) Handcuff

CHAPTER 2

BEHAVIORAL PSYCHOLOGY: YOU ARE YOUR OWN WORST ENEMY

Question: Do you tend to buy high and sell low?

Headwind 1: Human Emotions

Every so often, financial services research firm Dalbar releases statistics comparing stock market returns to the average investor's actual returns (dependent on when the investor buys and sells). The results of their studies are always the same. The average investor significantly trails the return of the market. Why is this the case? Investors buy when markets are up, when they feel comfortable and have added confidence in the market. They sell when the market is down and declines become too painful. In other words, they buy high and sell low.

In their 2011 study, Dalbar found for the twenty-year period ending on December 31, 2011, the average equity investor's annualized return was 3.49 percent. Meanwhile, the S&P 500 Index annualized return was 7.81 percent, and thus the common investor underperformed the S&P 500 by 4.32 percent for the past twenty years on an annualized basis.

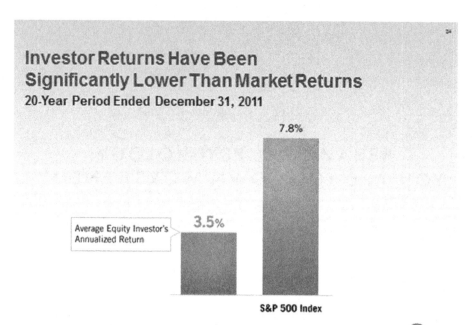

The Dalbar study makes a very strong case for buy-and-hold. After all, if these investors had invested their money without looking at their statements for twenty years, they would have more than doubled their annual average return. In a vacuum, the concept works. In reality, it may be more difficult to implement than we would like to admit. In other words, this approach is simple in theory, but its long-term execution is difficult in reality.

The problem is that buy-and-hold is analgous to telling overweight people who want to shed some pounds that the solution is easy and simple; they should eat no more than one thousand calories, and they should run for thirty minutes every day. This solution is simple in theory, but very difficult or nearly impossible to execute, as it is in our nature to occasionally deviate or crave variety.

Therefore, let's concede that one solution to the issue raised in Dalbar's research is to have a balanced portfolio and to follow a buy-and-hold strategy. You should choose your asset mix and not chase returns. Like Ron Popeil's classic rotisserie oven informercial slogan, you should "set it and forget it." Yes, the volatility in the markets may send you on a wild ride, but if you can avoid tinkering with your portfolio and chasing returns, you will be better off down the road.

Knowing the results of the study you might be saying, "All I have to do is select my balanced portfolio and not touch it for many years. Are you telling me that studies prove that this is a winning strategy that will produce above-average returns compared to my peers? It's a done deal. Sign me up."

Well, not so fast. Let's return to the diet analogy from above. Just because the instructions are simple doesn't mean that the plan is easy to implement over a long period of time. After all, we are human beings, not unemotional androids.

Before we address other headwinds that investors face, such as investment ignorance and the current economic environment, we need to first take a look in the mirror. We need to first recognize the powerful forces that influence human decision making. **Whether we decide to implement a theoretically simple game plan like buy-and-hold or more hands-on strategies, good strategies are useless if we cannot stick to them.** If we let specific behavioral tendencies get the best of us, we may be no better off than the investors cited in the Dalbar study, who wing it with little discipline or direction.

To avoid falling victim to such tendencies, the first thing we need is awareness.

Psychological Hurdles

1. **Loss Aversion:** Studies like those that Daniel Kahneman discusses in his book *Thinking, Fast and Slow* indicate that people on average possess a "loss-aversion ratio" of 1.5 to 2.5 times. For example, if you were to put one hundred dollars on the flip side of a coin, most people would request to be paid $150 to $250 to take part in that bet, in return for potentially losing their one hundred dollars. We can conclude from studies like this that the pain of loss is roughly twice as great as the pleasure of gain.

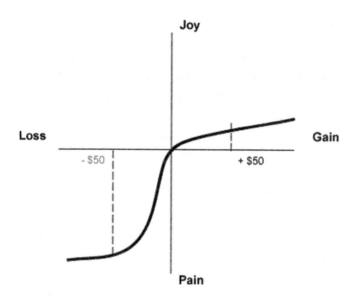

Copyright © 2007 Investopedia Inc.

This function is a representation of the difference in pain or joy that is achieved as a result of a certain amount of gain or loss. It is essential to note that not everyone's value function would look exactly like this; this graph represents more of an average. The most evident feature is how a loss creates a greater feeling of pain compared to the joy that an equivalent gain creates. For example, the absolute joy of finding fifty dollars is a lot less than the absolute pain of losing fifty dollars.

The above example is extremely important because when it comes to investing, you are putting up your hard-earned money. I suggest that portfolios should be tailored to individual investors so that they will be comfortable enough with the regular fluctuations (volatility) so that they won't be emotionally driven to sell before reaching their goal. As we will soon evaluate, risk tolerance is equivalent to pain threshhold. At what point in a portfolio decline does the emotional pain become too much to bear? When tailoring a portfolio, it is imperative that we honestly self-evaluate and know when this tipping point is reached. Why? Because if you blindly commit to a portfolio (including a sixty–forty balanced portfolio) and experience some downside volatiltiy past your tipping point, the impulse to sell (and scrap buy-and-hold) may be more powerful than you bargained for.

In order to head off imprudent, emotional financial decisions, better self-assessment and more downside awareness in portfolios need to be incorporated.

Playing defense and being risk aware (risk of loss in portfolio) is more in line with most people's risk tolerance than playing just offense (since the pain of loss is twice as great).

Read more here: http://www.investopedia.com/university/behavioral_finance/behavioral11.asp#ixzz2KzChDErs.

2. **Volatility:** An eye-opening statistical trend is that we have now entered an era of dramatically increased levels of volatility, or fluctuations in price.

> If we were to examine the number of 3 percent (up or down) daily moves in the S&P 500 Index over the past six decades, we would find that we have experienced more volatile moves in the past decade than the previous five decades combined! (Source: Yahoo Finance)

Therefore, it has become increasingly harder for individuals to fend off their human emotions and rationally invest as volatility has increased. This problem is akin to extreme turbulence during air travel, which is enjoyable to almost no one.

There is no doubt that volatility has been amplified in recent years. This is definitely due in part to technological advances that make it easier to trade, which has led to super computers conducting high-frequency trades (HFTs). What does this mean to the average investor? It means that emotions will be intensified as accounts can fluctuate faster and swing further than before. Increased volatility causes you to push your emotional fear and greed buttons harder and more frequently. This is not conducive to buy-and-hold for emotional investors. Large declines in the price of an investment makes it more difficult for many investors to sit still or stay the course. As we noted, loss aversion is approximately twice as painful as a gain, and volatility increases the odds that an investor will see a decline (even if temporary) that may trigger some emotional pain.

3. **Anchoring:** Adding to the issues of volatility and loss aversion is the behavioral bias of anchoring. This is the tendency to use an idea or fact as a reference point for future decision making, even though these reference points have no bearing on future judgments or decisions.

   For example, suppose an individual purchased a home in 2000 for $300,000. At the peak of the housing market in 2007, the home had appreciated to $750,000, but the individual did not sell. In 2013, the homeowner learned that the current value of the home was $600,000. The individual is now ready to sell his or her home.

   If the homeowner views this transaction as a $150,000 loss ($750,000 to $600,000), he or she has thus anchored onto its peak value in 2007, and this might prevent him or her from accepting a fair current market offer. Contrary to anchored beliefs, if the homeowner were to sell the home today, there would be a gain of $300,000, not a loss of $150,000.

   Similarly, investors check their statements on a regular basis. In a volatile environment, they might anchor onto a statement that was high one month. They might then react negatively to a subsequent monthly statement that shows a temporary decline in values due to volatility. Self-induced anchoring only clouds one's judgment, which leads to emotional decisions and imprudent actions. This can lead to poor results. All of this is more likely to occur with increased levels of volatility.

4. **Action Bias:** Action bias is the opposite of patience. It refers to the need or desire to execute buys and sells within

one's account (not buy-and-hold). As James Montier points out in *The Little Book of Behavioral Investing*, "Part of the problem for investors is that they expect investing to be exciting, largely thanks to the bubble vision." The influence of technology, whether it is TV or the Internet, has led to a regularly declining length of holding period for stocks. The average holding period of a stock has fallen from eight years in the 1960s to around five days today (Source: LPL Financial).

www.businessinsider.com/stock-investor-holding-period-2012-8

People want activity. It makes them feel as though they are being productive and taking action. Montier points out that "the bias to action is especially noteworthy—the urge to act tends to intensify after a loss—a period of poor performance, in portfolio terms." Therefore, the human urge to sell when the account is down is a huge obstacle to overcome. Dalbar points out that most people cannot overcome this urge. Investors often anchor to higher values that decline due to increased volatility. With declining values, loss aversion, and action bias, investors often sell at the wrong time. All of this makes buy-and-hold very challenging.

5. **Herding**:
   When we decide to take action, we have to be careful that we are buying and selling at the right time and for the right reasons. However, we may find that we are simply following the advice of friends or family, or maybe we are reacting to the local news.

Side note: As social animals, we feel more comfortable following the herd and doing what others are doing. It is amusing to run financial plans for families with financial situations all across the financial spectrum. A good number of families aren't sure if their current game plan is sound. They often want to know what their peers are doing and compare themselves to them (to the herd). That is very reassuring to many people. "How much do you want to live on in retirement?" This is a common and admittedly difficult question to answer. Many people have no idea how to answer it. Oftentimes they reply by asking, "What do most people say?" It is amusing because we are trying to tailor a game plan to them, yet they want it tailored to the average or norm. This defeats the purpose a bit.

When it comes to investments, many people rush into stocks when everyone is getting in, and they do this when markets have already risen. They want to get out when the numbers show that people are getting out, and they do this when markets have already fallen. Unfortunately for the small investor, the average American gets in and out at the wrong time. Pictures speak a thousand words, and the next graph does a great job reinforcing this claim. The chart illustrates the flow of investors' money into equity (stock) funds and bond funds. The circled areas show how the highest amounts of flows into stock funds were at the peak of the market in 1999. In other words, when stock prices were peaking, so was the individual (the average, small) investors' optimism and the amount they were investing into stock mutual funds. Conversely, the lowest amount of flows into stock funds was in 2008 and 2009. This occurred at the bottom of the market. This is a graphical way of expressing the phenomena of small investors buying high (1999) when the market is expensive as opposed to buying low (2008, 2009) when the market is inexpensive.

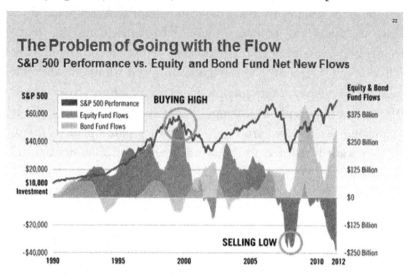

With hindsight, wouldn't you have liked to do the exact opposite of the herd? Wouldn't you have wanted to sell in 2000 and buy in 2009? Again, this would have been extremely difficult to execute at the time, but the chart shows that the correct action would have been to go against the consensus of your peers.

Montier also notes that neuroscientists have studied brain activity when subjects go either with or against the group in various scenarios. He explains that nonconformity and conflicted thinking lit up the amygdala, which is the brain's center for emotional processing and fear. In addition, studies showed that social exclusion generated brain activity in the anterior cingulated cortex and the insula, both of which are also activated by real physical pain. Montier concludes, "**Doing something different from the crowd is the investment equivalent of seeking out social pain.** As a contrarian investor, you buy the stocks that everyone else is selling, and you sell the stocks that everyone else is buying. This is social pain. The pyschological results suggest that following such a strategy is like having your arm broken on a regular basis. It's not fun!"

Contrarion Indicators (Going Against the Herd)

What if you could analyze the consensus of the herd in real time? As the Dalbar study and money flow chart both indicate, average investor often make the wrong decisions as to when to buy and sell. What if we could tap into other investors' psyches and gauge their level of optimism and pessimism? Would that provide you with valuable input regarding potential action you should be taking (i.e., the opposite or contrarian stance)?

Interestingly enough, many market analysts actually use the current mentality of the herd as a contrarian indicator to help determine when markets are under- or overbought. In other words, when the general consensus (herd mentality) is bullish, it may be time to be bearish and vice versa.

> The use of "**bull**" and "**bear**" to describe markets comes from the way the animals attack their opponents. A bull thrusts its horns up into the air while a bear swipes its paws down. These actions are metaphors for the movement of a market. If the trend is up, it's a bull market. If the trend is down, it's a bear market. —*Investopedia*

The American Association of Investors (AAII) has been tracking investor sentiment for many years, determining whether investors are optimistic, indifferent, or pessimistic on the direction of the stock market. These sentiments are also known as bullish, neutral, and bearish.

On the AAII website (http://www.aaii.com/sentimentsurvey) you will see updated sentiment readings. An example of what you might find will look something like this:

BULLISH: 42.3 percent
NEUTRAL: 29.0 percent
BEARISH: 28.7 percent

Having run these polls since 1987, AAII has gathered a lot of data and is able to analyze with hindsight sentiment readings with specific turning points in the market. What they have found is that these sentiment readings are strong contrarian indicators. When the majority is bullish, a bear market may be around the corner, and when everyone is bearish, a bull market may not be too far behind.

For example, before the famous Black Monday decline of 1987, there were very few investors that were bearish at the time, only 6 percent of those polled. On the flip side, before the market turned from bear to bull in 1990, a very high percentage of those polled were bearish (67 percent) after the Iraqi invasion of Kuwait. The conclusion many have come to is that we, the investors, should become very attentive to when bullish or bearish sentiments reach extremes.

In a research paper for AAII, Wayne A. Thorpe, CFA, drew the following conclusion:

"While little may be gleaned from changes in investor sentiment, identifying extreme levels of positive or negative sentiment appears to offer a glimpse of where the markets may be headed. In looking at the AAII Member Sentiment survey, we found that when sentiment reached overly bullish levels, the markets normally responded negatively in the months that followed. Conversely, the market tended to rise when members became overly bearish.

"While our results here seem to lend validity to the notion that investor sentiment may be used as a contrarian indicator, it would not be wise to base all your investment decisions upon it. Indicators such as this are best used in tandem with others so that you receive confirming signals of potential market movements. Sentiment merely serves as an additional tool when making investment decisions.

"Lastly, even if you do not use sentiment data as an indicator, it is a good idea to be mindful of it. As investors become overly bullish or overly bearish, it is easy to get caught up in the 'herd mentality.' However, as we have shown, if you run with the herd, you might get trampled."

Wayne A. Thorpe highlights that sentiment readings are just one signpost for the potential future directions of the market. An investor should utilize these readings as just one of many tools to evaluate the markets. However, the most interesting aspect of this indicator is that it is contrarian and it goes against what we, the average investing public, would intuitively assume the signals would indicate. **The herd is often wrong, and you can use that to your advantage!**

Another invaluable contrarian indicator is the Commitments of Traders (COT) reports that are published on a weekly basis. The COT reports show the positions of different traders in various markets, typically at the close of Tuesday's trading session. The Commodity Futures Trading Commission (CFTC), a US government body with the task of overseeing futures markets, prepares the report. The report's goal is to create transparency and to fight market manipulation, but it also serves as an an excellent read on the sentiment of the herd. The charts are valuable because they break down the market into three major categories: the commercials, the large speculators, and (as they are labelled) the "nonreportables," the small individual investors like you and me. Of these three, the two we want to focus on are the commercials, which are known as smart money, and the nonreportables, also known as the dumb money (i.e., the herd, or the public).

The COT data is my favorite contrarian indicator because with retrospection we can look back on various moves in different markets, and we can define specifically who was buying and who was selling at the time. The COT reports provide the clearest example of how the average public investor is suseptible to herd mentality and tends to buy and sell at the wrong time.

Notably, these charts provide indispensable feedback because they show what the herd, or dumb money, is doing. Equally as useful is the fact that these charts report the activity of smart money, or commercial/institutional money. This provides us with a double confirmation on these trades.

The website I utilize for COT analysis is www.COTbase.com. They have provided me with numerous charts that exhibit classic small investor behavior. However, we only need to examine one example to easily grasp the dynamics that are at play. On the next page you will find a COT chart for trading information regarding the price movements of the euro, which is a traded currency.

On the upper chart, you will see the market movements of the euro. Below that, you will see the trading activity of the commercials represented by the darker line on the middle chart. Below them, you will see the nonreportables (small investors) on the bottom chart. In looking at these two lines, the key is to identify movements up or down, which indicate their respective purchasing levels for that specific week.

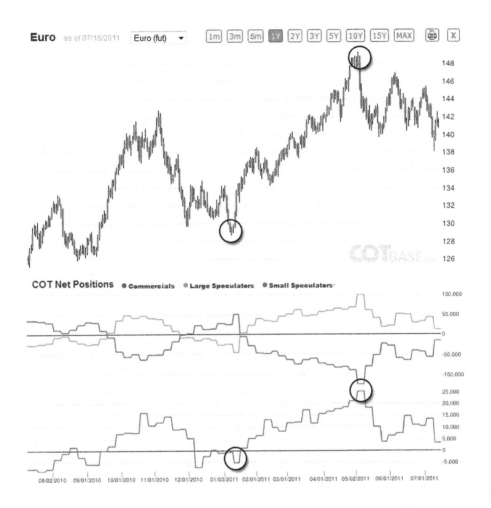

Chart provided by: COTbase.com

What the graph demonstrates is how the smart money and the dumb money were acting like synchronized swimmers, perfectly reflecting each other's moves at key turning points. Unfortunately for small investors, they were selling and buying at the wrong times. In early 2011, not only were the commercials buying at an elevated level, but the small investors were selling at a high level (represented by the first circled area, going left to right). This occurred right before the price went up. In May of that year, the opposite happened right before a price decline (represented by the second circled area).

Having to fend off psychological biases and to combat the wiring of the human neurological system is no small task. How do we overcome these tendencies? One option would be to attempt a buy-and-hold strategy. This can be easy if you utilize the ostrich technique of putting your head in the ground by never looking at your statements or turning on CNBC. Another option would be to invest in some sort of less liquid strategy, in which you have little say, control, or access to the funds. This might be a private placement or a hedge fund. A third option would be to utilize proactive tactical strategies that allow you to play both offense and defense in both bull and bear markets (tackling loss aversion). Therefore, you are less prone to the uncomfortable helplessness in major market declines where you see the value of your statement declining while Wall Street instructs you to do nothing (which triggers anchoring and the action bias).

Many of these proactive strategies can also reduce the volatility of your portfolio, thus preventing your pain threshold (risk tolerance) from being reached, causing panic selling. By reducing the opportunity for emotions to dictate your portfolio decisions (characteristics of common investor), your odds of success have dramatically increased.

A Summary of the Buy-and-Hold Strategy:
- It works best when implemented at market lows.
- It works best if you are not emotional.
- It may not work that well in the future (for reasons outlined in subsequent chapters).

Ultimately, we all have three basic choices:

1. **No Game Plan (Winging It).** I would submit to you that this leads to long-term underperformance that is similar to those studies published by Dalbar.
2. **Buy-and-Hold (In-the-Box).** For reasons we outline in this chapter, this strategy is harder to implement than you might think. For reasons we outline in chapter four, this may not be the most efficient strategy moving forward.
3. **Proactive but Disciplined Game Plan (Outside-the-Box).** These are less conventional options that we will outline throughout the book.

After reading the rest of this book, you should come to your own conclusion. However, if you do not make a personal choice, you indirectly have made a choice by default. This is option one. Unfortunately, this is the unconscious selection that many investors make. As statistics indicate, this isn't the most optimal choice. On the other hand, and fortunately for us, through the use of contrarian indicators, we can actually use the unconsciousness of the herd to our advantage.

In summary
- Research has shown that individual investors tend to inhibit their long-term returns by buying and selling at less than ideal times.
- Psychological behavior analysis helps us understand some of the triggers that cause poor performance in trading behavior.
- To better avoid poor performance, we need to first understand how we process information, how we emotionally react, and how we make decisions.

Be Fearful When Others Are Greedy and Greedy When Others Are Fearful.

—Warren Buffett

CHAPTER 3

COMMON MISCONCEPTIONS ABOUT CONVENTIONAL INVESTING

Question: When you chose your 401(k) investment options, did you select the options that most recently performed the best? Did you assume that those funds had more talented investment managers?

Headwind 2: Investment Ignorance

The most common investment accounts used to save for college and retirement are 529 college savings plans and 401(k)s or 403(b)s. The most common investment vehicles within these accounts are mutual funds. Due to the widespread availability and usage of mutual funds, it is important that you understand specific characteristics and nuances before we introduce our recommendations.

Here are the common misconceptions that we see people have regarding the operations and objectives of mutual funds:

1) Many people misunderstand what motivates and guides the investment decisions and performances of many mutual fund managers.
2) Many people, especially within employer-sponsored retirement accounts, are not as diversified as they are led to believe. In other words, their stock holdings are highly correlated; if one investment goes down, they all go down.

3) Many people do not hold portfolios that are truly tailored to their unique personal risk tolerance. Rather, they hold portfolios that others deem suitable for someone their age.

To best understand the value and importance of the recommendations in this book, it is imperative that we clarify these misconceptions!

Misconception 1: People misunderstand the motivations driving the investment decisions and performances of many mutual fund managers.

What is a managed mutual fund?

A mutual fund is an investment vehicle that is made up of a pool of funds that many investors collect to invest in securities, such as stocks, bonds, money market instruments, and similar assets. Money managers operate mutual funds. They invest the fund's capital and attempt to produce capital gains and income for the fund's investors. **A mutual fund's portfolio is structured and maintained to match the investment objectives stated in its prospectus.**—*Investopedia*

I highlighted the last line of the mutual fund definition because I have witnessed many investors incorrectly assuming that they know what each mutual fund's objective is. These assumptions often lead to confusion, frustration, and disappointment. You know how the saying goes—when you assume, it makes an "ass" out of "u" and "me." The following information is important because it helps lay the foundation for many of the recommendations found throughout the second half of this book. For example, why in certain instances we may not want to use mutual funds while in other instances we do, but very specific types.

A few decades ago, if you wanted to invest in the market, you could call up your broker on the phone and ask to purchase some stocks that she or her brokerage house had recommended at the time. As time went on, easier solutions were created by Wall Street to help the average investor gain access to the markets (i.e., the mutual fund). This is where you, the investor, pools your money with other investors and hire a manager to make investment decisions. This is accomplished by buying shares in their mutual fund. In addition to having an "expert" oversee your portfolio, another benefit was that these funds would often hold a couple hundred positions, providing all the shareholders with instant diversification. The risk that a single bankruptcy would threaten an entire account would be negligible. Furthermore, even though one had exposure to hundreds of companies, the money would remain extremely liquid. One sell order would need to be placed, and by the end of the day, the mutual fund shares would be converted into cash. The convenience and value these vehicles provided to the common investor led to a booming industry.

The benefits of managed mutual funds are as follows:

1. **Professional management**
2. **Instant diversification**
3. **Liquidity**

As a result of increasing popularity, the menu of fund types expanded, and with increasing options, funds became more compartmentalized. The industry began to emphasize asset-class-specific funds, such as large-cap, small-cap, international funds, and even further subsets of each. The marketing enacted was to promote "style-pure" funds that wouldn't deviate from their unique classification niche.

In other words, managers running large-cap US stock funds would be met with criticism by management and rating services if they were to buy too many mid caps, or international companies (as an example). The idea was that a well-designed, tailored portfolio would have specific percentages of each asset class. If managers deviated too far from the mandate, it would misalign individual investors' asset allocations, unknowingly overexposing them to one asset class and underexposing them to another (i.e., you don't need or want your large-cap manager giving you more exposure to small-cap stocks, as you already have a percentage of your portfolio allocated to that).

Ironically, the unintended consequence of this evolution in the fund industry was that it diminished the value of hiring professional mutual fund managers. By constricting the investment choice, their talent of choosing good investments became limited to fewer and fewer companies. As a result, mutual fund managers became niche stock pickers focusing only on the specific category they were assigned to.

Herein births the misaligned assumptions made by many investors. They assume that the purpose of hiring a manager, and the reason why some get labeled as a "good fund," is because of the manager's talent in choosing investments. Furthermore, they may assume that the manager's objective is to maximize returns every year by selecting the best ideas from the entire universe of potential investments. In other words, manage the fund as if it was their own money.

The actual goal of the manager is very much different from that outlined above. The objective of most funds is to manage risk and return compared to a corresponding index (or aforementioned subsets of the market). Large-cap managers compare themselves to a large-cap index, small-cap managers to a small-cap index, international, real estate, corporate bond, etc.

What is an index?

An index is a list of stocks (or other investment) that represents a portion of the overall market. Each index has an identifiable number of companies that fit its profile. For example, there is a large-cap index, a small-cap index, etc.

The question that the financial services industry has been struggling with for years is the question of: is it better to own a low-cost, passive index fund rather than owning a more expensive managed fund? Surely with the proliferation of managed mutual funds, managers must be able to add value to the individual investor to compensate for their management fees. Surely the vast majority of them must be able to outperform their respective indexes. After all, the indexes just represent a collection of stocks, they aren't hand-picked and monitored the way a managed fund is.

Question: Is it possible that owning the index provides equal value to hiring an expert to sort through and filter out his or her best picks?

Vanguard's paper *The Case for Indexing*, which can be found on its website, begins by stating, "The clear objective of actively managed portfolios is to outperform a given benchmark." Herein lies the issue that Main Street has with Wall Street. The mutual fund industry has gotten so compartmentalized that you can rarely hire a manager for a stock mutual fund who has free rein to invest in his or her best ideas or what he or she may view as the most attractive asset class, given current market conditions. Rather, he or she may be managing, for example, one of nine subsets of the domestic equity (US stock) exposure. There are value, blend, and growth managers for large, medium, and small companies (nine style boxes and nine indices), not including very small microcap companies.

*Note: In order to best comprehend Vanguard's study, we need to sidestep our conversation for a moment to get a quick primer on the nine primary style boxes and corresponding indexes.

	Value	Blend	Growth
Large			
Mid			
Small			

General guidelines of categories:

Large: Companies with a market capitalization value of more than ten billion dollars.

Mid: Companies with a market capitalization of two billion to ten billion dollars.

Small: Companies with a market capitalization of fewer than two billion dollars.

Growth: A growth company usually does not pay a dividend, as the company would prefer to reinvest retained earnings in capital projects. Most technology companies are growth stocks. Quite often, a growth company's stock is considered overvalued. The appeal of these companies is positive momentum/innovation and promising prospects in the future. Therefore, many investors are willing to pay a high price given a company's current earnings (e.g., Amazon.com).

Value: A value company tends to trade at a lower price in relation to its fundamentals (i.e., dividends, earnings, sales, etc.), and thus the stock (given its price) can often be considered undervalued.

Blend: Some combination of growth and value companies.

In *The Case for Indexing*, Vanguard analyzed the total performance of the nine stock styles of both managed and passive indexes over the fifteen years ending on December 31, 2011. Note, the study did include failed funds (funds that closed and are no longer operating) as part of its data set and thus part of the group that didn't beat the benchmark over that time period. Here is what Vanguard reports:

Over the fifteen years the respective indexes outperformed the following percentages of actively managed funds in each category:

> Large-Cap Value: 57 percent
> Large-Cap Blend: 84 percent
> Large-Cap Growth: 75 percent
> Mid-Cap Value: 100 percent
> Mid-Cap Blend: 96 percent
> Mid-Cap Growth: 97 percent
> Small-Cap Value: 70 percent
> Small-Cap Blend: 95 percent
> Small-Cap Growth: 78 percent

Granted, not every fund has been in existence for fifteen years. Even still, the numbers are pretty dramatic. The data makes a strong case against hiring a manager to gain exposure to subsets of the market and for simply purchasing the low-cost, unmanaged index funds.

This brings us to the crux of the matter. What is the mutual fund manager's ultimate objective? Is it to choose the best stocks from the entire universe of listed companies? Is it to attempt to achieve consistent positive returns for investors? No. **The mutual fund manager's goal is to attempt to outperform its benchmark or index. What in the world does that mean to the average American?** Now, managers may still want to choose the best companies that are available to them, but their universe is limited to the mandate of their prospectuses. If a manager of a large-cap fund thinks that the best opportunities are in small caps or even bonds, then unfortunately his or her hands are tied.

An acquaintance of mine who is in the industry shared with me that in addition to the style mandates that handcuff managers, the incentive structure may also be to blame for the industry's underperformance. Managers with average performances are rarely fired. Therefore, they are able to keep their hefty salary year in and year out, and it may be in their interest to somewhat mimic the index, or own the same companies as the index. This would prevent major underperformance (i.e., lagging the index and their peers dramatically), which wouldn't be good for job security.

Montier echoes the same point, stating, "The vast majority of professional investors simply don't try to arbitrage against bubbles because of self-serving bias and myopia. They are benchmarked against an index and fear underperforming that index above all else (aka career risk); thus they don't have the appetite to stand against bubbles. This is amplified by the fact that most fund management organizations are paid on the basis of assets under management, so the easiest way of not getting fired is to deliver a performance close to the benchmark (aka business risk). These two elements of self-serving bias collude to prevent many managers from 'doing the right thing.'"

Many mutual fund managers do not get paid to always invest in their best ideas or sidestep major market crashes. Rather, they get paid to outperform a benchmark!

Problem: You should not assume that all fund managers are investing your money as if it was their own, are fully utilizing their talent, are choosing their best ideas. These false assumptions can lead to an unfortunate decision making process following a period of poor performance. The average investor may be inclined to sell and purchase a better recent performer because the assumption is that the better performer must have a more talented and skilled manager. Essentially, this behavior breeds the common culprit of chasing returns (buying high), but really just the hot asset class (the true driver of performance).

We want to stress that not all funds operate this way, but unfortunately the vast majority of them do. As we will point out in chapter eight, a handful of unique and unconstrained mutual funds are not handcuffed by restrictive policies. The key is to be aware of such strategies. In the next chapter, we will address why it is so important to find them.

Therefore, if most managed funds cannot outperform their respective index over time, and hiring a manager carries an expense, why not just invest in indexes? Herein lies the argument for indexing and placing less value on hiring a mutual fund manager.

It is worth noting that by outlining the virtues of Vanguard's arguments, I am not necessarily knocking the skills of fund managers. Instead, it is more so a critique of the system that they have to play in (a system the common investor is unaware of). I believe that many managers, if left to their own expertise, can identify excellent stocks and bonds for purchase. However, when a prospectus requires that holdings cannot exceed a couple percent of the total portfolio (thus diluting the impact of their highest conviction picks), and it restricts the types of companies that they can purchase by various characteristics, talents will undoubtedly be muted.

The situation is analogous to that of a baseball manager who needs to field a team but can only select from a pool of second basemen to play all nine positions. It will most certainly be challenging for that manager to produce stellar results.

Keep in mind that many mutual fund managers have to deal with several headwinds to outperformance.

- Expenses. Trading costs, salaries for the management team, and salaries for the research analysts are all necessary, but they detract from the fund's total performance numbers.
- According to the prospectus, weightings of individual holdings may be capped at a percentage of the overall portfolio. For example, perhaps no security can make up more than 5 percent of the total portfolio. To clarify, this is not to say that these risk measures are good or bad in terms of risk-management policy. However, in terms of performance, it does force managers to hold numerous positions—typically hundreds of them. This inherently dilutes the value of their talent or their best ideas. The more diversified a fund becomes, the more it mirrors an index.
- A good percentage of fund managers are handcuffed, and they have a very select pool of investments to choose from (e.g., only small companies, only large companies, etc.). In addition, they often must remain within a specific asset class (stocks, bonds, cash, real estate, commodities, etc.). Therefore, even if managers spot opportunities outside of their strategy's niche focus, there is nothing they can do about that. Their hands are tied.
- According to the prospectus, many funds have to be fully (or close to fully) invested at all times. They have to be **all offense and no defense!** If managers of funds see a major bear market developing, they cannot proactively get defensive. For example, they cannot dramatically increase the cash positions.
- Career Risk. Ironically, being average often provides job stability and a healthy annual salary. If managers gamble

by trying to greatly outperform the benchmark/index, their plan could backfire. Even if they occur for just a year or two, large underperformance numbers can put a manager's salary and benefits at risk. For this reason, many managed funds resemble or closely mirror their respective benchmark/index (aka "closet index fund").

*Note: The prospectus mandates are there to help protect the shareholders. However, the handcuffing managerial rules dramatically diminish the value of decision making talent and justification as to why someone would pay managerial fees.

After you factor in expenses, diversification, constraint of investments and asset classes, and the career risk for veering too far away from the benchmark, it becomes extremely challenging to provide consistent outperformance of the index. Amazingly, this is the exact value that many fund companies have been selling for years. Unfortunately, **I think that they are misaligned with the needs and desires of their customers. The average investor is more interested in risk-controlled growth than a highly rated mid-cap growth fund that has outperformed its benchmark in three of the past four years.**

The restraints that the industry has imposed on managers have eliminated much of their value-add proposition. This is analogous to buying a Ferrari with the intention of being able to reduce the travel time of your daily commute. Considering the speed limits, you will unfortunately find that you have paid extra for a good vehicle, but your average travel time has not changed, and you could have purchased another car at a fraction of the cost. Great vehicle, but the system constrains the value it can add.

An investment theme found throughout the solutions chapters of this book is to invest in what you know. Unfortunately, ignorant investing often leads to poor results. I have seen too many investors make false assumptions regarding their investment funds, only to wind up confused and disappointed. Therefore, it is imperative that we lay the proper foundation to better help you understand the true nature of various investment funds options. This understanding will help you appreciate the rationale and provide you with added confidence in the specific investment vehicles recommended later in the book.

Introduction to the Exchange Traded Fund, or ETF

As a continuation of the previous discussion, it is important to introduce the increasingly popular exchange traded fund, or ETF for short. ETFs have become the next generation of fund investing.

Over time, many industries change with advances in technology that are geared for easier access, easier use, and increased functionality. The music industry used to sell records, tapes, and compact discs, and now they sell MP3s.

Similarly, the investment world has seen some evolution as well from broker to mutual fund to index mutual fund to the somewhat young exchange traded fund, or ETF. This doesn't suggest that the previous generation of investment vehicles are obsolete. However, there have been evolutionary steps with regard to investment ownership options for the average investor. A vehicle with lower than average expenses, increased transparency, and added liquidity has been birthed.

ETFs are closely related to mutual funds and even more so to index mutual funds, as most are not actively managed. Compared to mutual funds, they do provide some unique advantages.

1. **Lower expenses.** Although the fees charged throughout the ETF universe will vary depending on the strategy, these fees are generally lower than those of mutual funds.

Mutual Fund/ETF Fees and Expenses

According to Morningstar Inc., the average of the most recent total operating expenses (or prospectus net expense ratio) among active US mutual funds, excluding load-waive share classes and active US exchange traded funds (ETFs), are as follows:

Fund Type	**Mutual Funds**	**ETFs**
US Large-Cap Stock:	1.31 percent	.47 percent
US Mid-Cap Stock:	1.45 percent	.56 percent
US Small-Cap Stock:	1.53 percent	.52 percent
International Stock:	1.57 percent	.56 percent
Taxable Bond:	1.07 percent	.30 percent
Municipal Bond:	1.06 percent	.23 percent

2. **Transparency.** With ETFs, an investor has a daily disclosure of what is held within the fund. On the other hand, mutual funds only have to disclose their holdings quarterly. If you are the type of investor who would like to know your exact exposure to companies like Apple or Enron, ETFs provide a definite advantage.

3. **Liquidity.** As long as the market is open, you can purchase or redeem shares of your ETFs. Mutual funds, on the other hand, only meet redemptions after the close of the market. The liquidity of mutual funds may be further restrictive if they have a penalty on frequent trading or early distribution.

4. **No minimums.** ETFs are more accessible to investors who have smaller amounts of money. Mutual funds often require a minimum investment for investors to gain access to the fund. ETFs only require that you purchase one share.

5. **Tax Efficiency.** Since mutual funds have to sell the investments within the fund to meet large redemption requests, the fund may incur capital gains. These capital gains get passed on to the fund holder. The additional trading that is required for the inner operations of the mutual funds makes them less tax efficient than ETFs, which don't need to manage for redemptions, as the investor simply sells the shares to market.

6. **Specific Currencies and Commodities.** At certain times, investors may seek exposure to specific target asset classes. For example, ETFs allow investors to have their money mirror the movements in a country's currency or even specific commodities like precious metals, oil, or natural gas.

7. **Increased Trading Flexibility.** One could use stop orders and limit orders in addition to short-selling ETFs, all of which are not available for mutual funds. This approach is similar to stock trading, and it is more appropriate for sophisticated investors.

> Definition of Stop Order: An order to buy or sell a security when its price surpasses a particular point. This ensures a greater probability of achieving a predetermined entry or exit price, and this either limits the investor's loss or locks in his or her profit. Once the price surpasses the predefined entry/exit point, the stop order becomes a market order.
>
> Definition of Limit Order: An order placed with a brokerage to buy or sell a set number of shares at a specified price or better. Limit orders also allow an investor to limit the length of time that an order can be outstanding before it is canceled.
>
> Definition of Short Selling: The sale of a security that is not owned by the seller or that the seller has borrowed. Short selling is motivated by the belief that a security's price will decline, thereby enabling someone to buy it back at a lower price to make a profit.

You can implement many of the strategies recommended in this book through ETFs. In addition, many of the recommended tactical mutual funds actually utilize ETFs within their portfolios. For all of the above reasons, it is important that you become more familiar with ETFs.

For a helpful resource for researching available ETFs, consider visiting: http://etfdb.com/etfs/.

> Remember: Having a better tool in your tool kit is just one aspect of better investing, but it is noteworthy nonetheless. Whether you are listening to your record, tape, CD, or MP3 player, nothing will play when the power goes out. Conversely, you might be using a mutual fund, an index fund, or an ETF for exposure to blue chip stocks. However, when a bear market like the one in 2008 strikes, they all go down.
>
> Mutual funds, index funds, and ETFs by themselves won't protect us from down markets. However, knowing which specific tools to turn to and how to best use them in the face of sucvh environments may. That is the skill set we will explore in the solutions chapters. A skill set you can either outsource or proactively implement on your own.

Conclusion: It is a mistaken belief to think that hiring a money manager through the purchase of a mutual fund means that the manager will at all times be investing in their best ideas from the entire universe of available investment options. More often than not, the manager will be selecting from a focused segment of the universe and will be managing to, and trying to outperform, an index. If your current portfolio is constructed from these types of funds, more often than not, you will be better off gaining exposure to your chosen asset classes through the use of a low cost index or exchange traded funds.

However, on the flip side managers can be well worth their management fee when they are less constrained by investment mandates and can implement tactical allocation strategies, as outlined in chapter eight.

Misconception 2: Many average investors think they are well diversified if they own various categories of stocks (large, medium, small, international)

Problem: You are not as protected through traditional diversification as you might think. The conventional wisdom behind diversification is that if you spread out your risk to numerous holdings and asset classes, they will all be moving up and down at different times, thus reducing the risk of a major decline in your portfolio. However, what if this isn't true? What if all of your investments are set up to move in sync with each other?

As we will examine, there is a good chance that all of your stock positions mirror each other's movements. If this is the case, you may not be as protected through conventional diversification. Thus if your large-cap fund declines, the odds are that your mid-cap fund will follow suit. How does that help you?

First, the Importance of Asset Allocation: Around 91.5 percent of an investor's return will be due to the specific asset classes that he or she invests in (e.g., large company stocks, government bonds, real estate, etc.), rather than any specific investment or fund he or she may choose. This lends further credence to the idea that choosing a specific fund manager for a specific asset class is less important than you might think. Rather, what is important is the asset class itself. This conclusion has led many pension and endowment funds to develop their strategies around sound asset allocation. Diversification through proper asset allocation is one of conventional wisdom's most common pieces of advice that it recommends to help investors reduce volatility.

The following chart shows the performance of a select list of asset classes from 1998 through 2012. The highest performing asset class is shaded for each given year. Spending a few minutes analyzing this chart will provide you with the following insights. One, there are more asset classes than you might have assumed. Two, performance numbers for asset classes will vary in any given year. Three, Israelsen noted in the last three columns the flaw of trying to chase performance by selecting the asset class from the previous year that performed the best. Again, I often witness people making this type of decision within their 401(k)s, but it also leads to massive underperformance (as the Dalbar study also indicated).

> **A four- or five-star fund rating (awarded by Morningstar) is highly rated compared to its peers within an asset class. The rating of the fund doesn't determine performance; the asset class it represents does! (That is, a one-star short-term bond fund would outperform a five-star large-cap growth fund in another bear market like 2008.)**

Over time, as certain asset classes underperform, the idea is that others will outperform. Thus the volatility (the standard deviation or risk) of your portfolio will decrease. Reducing volatility is perhaps undervalued because with increased volatility comes the potential for irrational investor behavior, which studies have shown can lead to the significant underperformance of the overall market. In theory, asset allocation alleviates a lot of these emotions by reducing the volatility of an overall portfolio.

Again, the challenge to investors, in order for this strategy to work best, requires unemotional commitment. After all, the reduced volatility is a result of something that is counterintuitive to many investors' mind-sets. In an efficient asset allocation, there most likely will always be an underperforming asset class providing little to no (perhaps negative) return. But remember, just because one asset class is down doesn't mean you should remove it from your portfolio; it may be a strong performer in the subsequent year as markets change.

Year	Large US Stock	Mid-Cap US Stock	Small Cap Value US Stock	Developed Non-US Stock	Emerging Non-US Stock	REIT	Natural Resources	Commodities	US Bonds	TIPS	Non-US Bonds	Cash	Investor Pick Best Asset Class Each Year	Performance Chaser Pick last year's best asset class	Equal Weighted Average of All 12 Asset Classes
1998	28.67	16.90	4.76	19.60	-18.00	-16.25	-14.61	-27.98	8.56	3.74	17.66	5.34	28.67	28.67	2.37
1999	20.37	15.29	3.35	26.55	61.81	-3.95	26.63	42.81	-0.94	2.19	-6.84	5.01	61.81	20.37	16.02
2000	-9.71	17.37	21.88	-14.46	-27.45	26.46	15.24	24.43	11.49	12.95	-3.29	6.29	26.46	-27.45	6.77
2001	-11.81	-0.90	13.70	-21.71	-2.73	12.45	-16.00	-8.68	8.31	7.68	-4.43	4.16	13.70	12.45	-1.66
2002	-21.55	-14.37	-14.20	-15.43	-7.29	3.85	-14.37	24.56	10.12	16.33	21.33	1.65	24.56	-14.20	-0.78
2003	28.16	35.14	37.19	39.68	57.88	35.77	34.73	25.84	3.98	8.18	17.64	0.90	57.88	25.84	27.09
2004	10.69	15.77	23.55	18.94	26.31	30.87	24.69	37.15	4.22	8.30	11.53	1.11	37.15	26.31	17.76
2005	4.86	12.50	6.28	13.32	32.25	11.64	35.63	30.87	2.30	2.59	-9.25	3.01	35.63	30.87	12.17
2006	15.80	9.99	19.23	25.88	29.20	33.49	16.17	16.02	4.21	0.18	6.78	4.88	33.49	16.17	15.15
2007	5.12	7.12	-6.92	9.89	37.32	-16.42	33.71	31.50	6.84	11.95	10.41	5.14	37.32	-16.42	11.31
2008	-36.70	-36.34	-32.33	-41.02	-52.29	-37.00	-42.89	-31.74	8.49	-0.55	4.21	2.77	8.49	-52.29	-24.62
2009	26.31	37.49	30.98	26.84	75.29	30.07	37.07	16.19	3.70	8.94	5.44	0.53	75.29	3.70	24.90
2010	15.04	26.26	25.11	8.25	19.44	28.42	23.35	11.90	6.25	6.13	3.82	0.06	28.42	19.44	14.50
2011	1.89	-2.16	-4.20	-12.26	-18.74	8.56	-7.80	-2.57	7.91	13.27	3.98	0.05	13.27	8.56	-1.01
2012	16.02	17.82	18.97	18.82	19.20	17.62	2.02	3.50	3.92	6.39	5.86	0.04	19.20	6.39	10.85
15-Yr Ave. Return	4.39	8.81	8.18	4.31	9.55	8.78	7.31	10.53	5.91	7.11	5.29	2.71	32.25	2.71	7.95
15-Yr Std Dev	19.07	18.70	18.64	22.61	36.05	21.62	24.42	22.47	3.29	5.01	9.10	2.25	18.87	23.7	12.76

*Source: Craig L. Israelsen, PhD, 7Twelve Portfolio, www.7TwelvePortfolio.com.

Most investors don't have detailed asset class analysis like that provided by Israelsen. Unfortunately, I believe a disservice is done when the average investor gets a watered-down version of asset allocation. Take for example the asset allocation tool courtesy of *Money* magazine, which can be found here: http://cgi.money.cnn.com/tools/assetallocwizard/assetallocwizard.html.

All you have to do is answer four questions. I answered these questions with the mentality of an average investor with a moderate to moderately aggressive risk tolerance (not conservative or aggressive). As a result, the recommended portfolio was this:

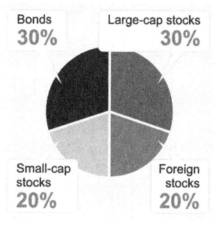

At first glance, most users of this tool would presumably assume it is a reasonable recommendation. It looks like a nice pie chart. It has different colors and is broken down into four different types of investments that we must assume provide adequate diversification. However, upon further investigation, this may not be true at all.

Running a ten-year correlation analysis reveals some surprising results. It shows that large, medium, small, and international don't offer the investor much in the way of diversification benefits. Using four Vanguard Index funds (S&P 500 for Large-Cap VFINX, Mid-Cap Index VIMSX, Small-Cap Index NAESX, and Total International Stock Index VGTSX), we can analyze how correlated one stock index is to another. If you compare one investment to itself as represented on the matrix, it will be a 1:1 correlation, or a 1.0. We find that the least correlated asset classes are small caps to international. That pairing still has a correlation of .86, which means that it is still highly correlated.

In the past, owning these different types of stock asset classes may have provided good diversification. That is no longer the case. If we head into a bear market for stocks, whatever percentages you allocated to small, medium, and large companies may matter very little, as they will most likely all decline. In other words, when one stock goes up, they all go up. When one goes down, they all go down. As the saying goes, "When the tides go out, all the boats sink."

	LC	MC	SC	INT
LC:	1	0.95	0.92	0.90
MC:	0.95	1	0.97	0.90
SC:	0.92	0.97	1	0.86
INT:	0.90	0.90	0.86	1

LC = Large-Cap Stocks
MC = Mid-Cap Stocks
SC = Small-Cap Stocks
INT = International Stocks

(Source: iShares Correlation Calculator, 2012 through 2012)

In the previous pie chart, we now know that 70 percent of this portfolio (which is allocated to various types of stocks) is highly correlated, and it provides little protection through diversification. So how can you do better and what should you consider for your own portfolio? To reduce the risk of volatility within portfolios, we need fewer correlated asset classes. To do this, we need to go beyond just stocks and bonds by adding a third core asset class: alternatives (discussed in chapters seven and ten). Therefore, I believe that basic asset allocation is not good enough anymore. It isn't good enough for the authors. It is not good enough for college endowment funds, which we will discuss later. It is also probably not good for you.

Points of Emphasis to the Individual Investor:

1. **There is now a high correlation between large, mid, small, and international stock indexes.** This can be very misleading when choosing your portfolio options within your work retirement plan. Choosing from limited options to begin with, the list of offerings provided under each of those four asset classes gives the investor the illusion of diversified investment choice. Unbeknownst to them, they may all produce similar results.
2. **The asset classes you choose for your portfolio matter much more than the fund manager or Morningstar rating.** If you are savvy with Morningstar or Yahoo Finance mutual fund filters, I challenge you to examine how many mid-cap or large-cap funds, for example, performed drastically different than their indexes in recent years. As you do these filters, it will become apparent how closely they all behave to each other.

Conclusion: In the past owning large-cap, mid-cap, small-cap, and international stock funds were believed to provide an investor with good diversification. This is no longer true.

Misconception 3: Many average investors do not hold portfolios that are truly tailored to their unique personal risk tolerance.

Problem: If investors are forced into portfolios based on rules of thumb that are not in line with their unique expectations, then if expectations aren't met, these misaligned objectives can lead to disappointments. This is typically followed by emotional responses, irrational decision making, and poor performance.

A mandatory first step to tailoring an investment portfolio is to complete a risk tolerance questionnaire. However, over time I have become increasing frustrated with how most are constructed and how investors interact with them. The three issues I encourage you to bring a little more awareness to when you complete your next questionnaire are: 1) time horizon, 2) personal honesty, and 3) realistic expectations.

1) **Time horizon:** To varying degrees, almost all questionnaires factor in the investor's time frame. When the time frame is longer, the recommended portfolio is more aggressive. I understand the logic here. The investor has more time to recover from a loss in the account. However, this philosophy to encourage increased stock exposure (aggressiveness) based on time frame assumes that the investor in not emotional and will not react following a market correction. Increasing stock exposure for someone who will panic and sell in a large decline is counterproductive. The investor winds up selling low and probably will only reenter the market after it has gone up again and become more expensive. This (piece of conventional wisdom) is precisely one of the cause and effect scenarios that lead to the underperformance numbers outlined by the Dalbar research paper.

> An analogy: If you wanted to travel from LA to New York, the conventional wisdom is that you should fly. However, what if you are like Hall of Fame football coach John Madden, who is terrified of flying? What if you, like Coach Madden, would be completely content to take a bus to your destination instead? Sure, it would take longer, but you would be comfortable and would be sure to arrive at your destination. Should your travel agent ignore your personal desires and force you onto a plane? This is analogous to your financial advisor risk forcing you into more aggressive investments simply because you indicated you have a longer time horizon than most.

2) **Personal Honesty:** When looking for some health advice from his doctor, Phil was asked how many alcoholic drinks he consumes per week, how often he exercises, and how many hours of sleep he gets per night. Phil responded with three or four drinks, three times per week, and eight hours per night.

Problem is Phil bent the truth a little for fear of being judged. Truth of the matter is Phil consumes closer to ten drinks per week, almost never exercises, and has trouble sleeping almost every other night.

Question is: Do you think the doctor will be able to tailor the best advice for Phil not knowing his true lifestyle?

I have often observed investors answering the risk tolerance questions as if it were a high school exam (repeating what you have been told). They don't honestly answer the questions; rather, they put down the answer that they know is most socially accepted (or consensus view). For example, if a question asks what you would do if the market declined by 30 percent, would you:

A) buy more

B) do nothing

C) sell and go to cash?

A good number of respondents will select B. (*Insert sarcasm.*) Of course they are not emotional; of course they wouldn't overreact to a decline on their statement. Almost never do they admit that in real life they may have sold and gone to cash, or shifted to something they thought was "safer," or chased returns and moved the money into an investment that was performing (i.e., followed their human instincts).

Just like Phil not being 100 percent truthful with his doctor, if you cannot commit to honest self-assessment, just like Phil you may not get the best advice. As an advisor I would prefer to know that you would want to sell and go to cash because I can better tailor my advice accordingly. I acknowledge that this exercise is not easy. However, in relation to constructing an efficient investment game plan, it is imperative.

3) **Realistic Expectations:** If you break down the term "risk tolerance," essentially it is asking you how much pain (risk) you can withstand (tolerance). It is not asking you how fast you want your portfolio to grow. Hence the third issue of unrealistic expectations.

News Flash: Everyone wants the same thing. Lots of consistent growth with no portfolio declines! Who wouldn't want that?

Many investors (overwhelmingly represented by one gender) interpret risk tolerance as a trap designed to slow down the potential appreciation of their portfolio. "I want to be aggressive!" However, when asked if we were to experience another year like 2008 when stocks were down almost 40 percent, how much of a decline would they be willing to withstand (aka risk tolerance), their answer is a fraction of that. Although this book does outline strategies that (we feel) come closer to this scenario of having our cake and eating it too, we also need to have more realistic expectations that with increased opportunity for appreciation comes increased opportunity for declines.

What I have found to be an effective way of addressing realistic expectations and grounding some of the investing Supermen who think they are invincible, is to focus on historical risk and return numbers.

What is one good way to better gauge one's true risk tolerance? We need to "get real" by utilizing real life return numbers.

1. **Q: Which portfolio is most appealing to you, given its 10-year average return and worst down year?**

		10-Yr	Down Yr
A)	_____	4.67%	-10.53%
B)	_____	5.42%	-19.52%
C)	_____	6.27%	-26.50%
D)	_____	6.74%	-34.39%
E)	_____	7.29%	-37.02%

    Statistics provided by Morningstar through December 31, 2013.

Option A represents the Vanguard LifeStrategy Income Fund (VASIX), categorized by Morningstar as a conservative allocation fund that is approximately 20 percent stocks, 80 percent bonds.

Option B represents the Vanguard LifeStrategy Conservative Growth Fund (VSCGX), categorized by Morningstar as a conservative allocation fund that is approximately 40 percent stocks, 60 percent bonds.

Option C represents the Vanguard LifeStrategy Moderate Growth Fund (VSMGX), categorized by Morningstar as a moderate allocation fund that is approximately 60 percent stocks, 40 percent bonds.

Option D represents the Vanguard LifeStrategy Growth Fund (VASGX), categorized by Morningstar as an aggressive allocation fund that is approximately 80 percent stocks, 20 percent bonds.

Option E represents the Vanguard 500 Index Fund (VFINX), categorized by Morningstar as a large-cap blend fund that is approximately 100 percent stocks, 0 percent bonds.

I believe that by referencing these five options and their statistics, it opens up a better, more tangible discussion around what one may expect on a return and risk scale given different levels of aggressiveness. For example, you indicated that you have a moderate risk tolerance. A typical moderate investor would have experienced a -26.50 percent one-year return on its way to achieving an average annual return of 6.27 percent. Therefore, with history providing us with expectations moving forward, if we were to encounter a similar bear market, would you be able to hold your portfolio through a similar down year? If not, then we should consider the next less aggressive option, and so on down the aggressiveness spectrum of options. Remember, an investor who sells at the bottom of the market will be way behind the eight ball toward his or her goals. We need to set proper expectations up front and commit to a game plan that will help us best avoid emotional/panic selling.

In addition to helping set proper expectations moving forward, it also helps you create your own fair benchmark for statistical comparison moving forward. Using the list of Vanguard funds as a historical reality check is a great conversation starter as to what you must be willing to endure (downside volatility) to achieve higher average annual returns as you move up the risk scale. These are low-cost index funds based on conventional wisdom asset allocation philosophies. They exhibit long track records and provide investors with concrete hard evidence as what to expect from allocation portfolios across the risk spectrum. These are not "what if" high-level philosophical questions found within some questionnaires. Conversely, this one multiple choice question encourages a simple three-step process: choose one answer, discuss, and commit.

What your personal benchmark shouldn't be is 100 percent in stocks during bull markets and 100 percent in cash during bear markets. By assuming you can conveniently flip-flop from one extreme to the other as markets change, you will have unrealistic expectations and will never win! Especially with no disciplined game plan. These are the folks chasing stocks late in a bull run and who also rush to cash late in a bear market: a rudderless ship.

Of course this is just the conversation starter in terms of expectations and desires. Before detailing an investment game plan it allows you, your spouse, advisor, etc., to all be on the same page. Unfortunately, many investors dive into portfolios with little to no self-assessment or realistic expectations. This is a recipe for disaster as chaotic emotional decisions are sure to eventually rear their ugly heads.

My personal belief is that a portfolio should rely less on the time frame and more on the personality of the investor, the investor's expectations, and the current market environment he or she is in. The bottom line with all investment options is that the more you understand what you are invested in, the more comfortable you will be with your selections. As a result, you will have more realistic expectations and experience less surprises, and thus make fewer poor investment decisions based on emotions. Ultimately your success will be determined by how effectively you can remain disciplined and true to whichever game plan you choose.

Conclusion: One of the worst decisions an investor can make is to sell based on emotion. This assures the investor to go to cash at the least opportune time. The best way to prevent this from occurring is to better assess one's pain threshold and develop an investment game plan that will evade that trigger point. On the flip side, an un-tailored game plan based primarily on one's timeframe possesses a much higher probability of exceeding that threshold and prompting an emotional sell decision. For the average investor, more honest risk tolerance assessments and better tailored portfolios are critical to long-term investment success.

> **In summary**
> The three common misconceptions that lead investors to invest less efficiently are as follows:
>
> 1. Misaligned goals between investors and money managers.
> 2. Poor portfolio diversification.
> 3. Portfolios that are not truly tailored to the investor.

These three factors have caused confusion among investors, and they have led to higher than desired levels of volatility. The good news is that we can address all three of these factors, and we will attempt to do so later in the book.

I never understood why underperforming a benchmark was a greater sin than losing money.

—Christopher Guptil, CIO and CEO of Broadmark Asset Management

CHAPTER 4

WHERE ARE WE AND WHERE ARE WE GOING?

Note: Some aspects of this chapter may appear dated as time passes. Since economic snapshots taken at specific moments in time are presented, this is unavoidable. Although this data may change through the years, the principles discussed in relation to them shouldn't.

Question: Many investors have faith in their buy-and-hold-balanced portfolio because it has always served them well in the past, and they assume this economic environment is no different. However, what if this time is different?

Headwind 3: Current economic environment

The five things you need to know and further motivation to consider out-of-the-box strategies:

1) **Debt**
2) **Deficits**
3) **Quantitative Easing (QE)**
4) **Inflation**
5) **Rising Rates**

Five important issues that investors and retirees must understand:

Oftentimes, you may turn on the business channel, glance at the business section of your local newspaper, or watch political debates and begin to tune out when financial terms are tossed about. However, there are certain topics and issues that I highly recommend you attempt to grasp, at least on a very basic level. Therefore, before we explore potential recommendations, let's first discuss our current economic environment. This will also help us explain the importance behind our recommendations in chapters six through eleven, and it will help provide you with some motivation to take action.

This decade might turn out to be very different from the previous decades, and you should approach your investment management accordingly. Since the current environment is different than ones in the past, rules of thumb, accepted universal theories, and conventional planning strategies may not work as efficiently as they used to. If you want to grow your money with less risk and increase your odds of successfully addressing your financial goals, please assimilate the following information.

As a side note, this chapter and its contents played a major role in motivating me to write this book. I feel it is extremely important for you (the reader) to spread, educate, and inform your peers about this information.

Your finances aren't very different from a corporation or government even though they are obviously on an entirely different scale. By drawing parallels with your own personal situation, the information might be easier to process. On a basic level, the finances of a household, a business, and the government operate in the same way. Each has income (cash flow in), expenses (cash flow out), assets, and liabilities (debts). Let's get a better understanding of these concepts by analyzing current data and charts.

Concept 1: Debt

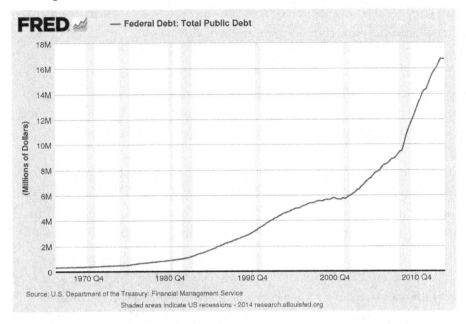

Data Source: FRED, Federal Reserve Economic Data, Federal Reserve Bank of St. Louis: *Federal Debt: Total Public Debt [GFDEBTN]*; US Department of the Treasury: Financial Management Service; http://research.stlouisfed.org/fred2/series/GFDEBTN; accessed February 19, 2014.

Real-time debt level calculations can be found here: http://www.usdebtclock.org/

The chart above shows the level of government debt at the time of writing this book. This debt has been rapidly rising for several years. The level of debt isn't necessarily an issue on its own, unless we compare it to the cash flow levels addressed in the next concept: surplus/deficit. For example, it may seem like a major problem for many of your peers to hear that a friend has $50,000 of credit card debt. However, when you subsequently learn that your friend makes $500,000 per year, you realize that major issues for some people aren't big problems for other people. Everything is relative, and debt levels—even increasing ones—need to be taken in context so that we can best understand their levels of threat.

However, what if your friend doesn't make $500,000 per year, but rather $8,000 per year and is carrying $50,000 in credit card debt (which happens to be close to the same ratio our government is at)? That situation is a whole different story.

Transitioning the discussion to the government's state of affairs, the story doesn't end there. The $17 trillion figure that is often mentioned for the current national debt does not include *unfunded liabilities*. These are future payment promises for which no current funding is available.

> **Unfunded Liabilities:** "The difference between the net present value of expected future government spending and the net present value of projected future tax revenue, particularly those associated with Social Security and Medicare." (Source: Forbes)

Forbes estimates this number to be in the $127 trillion range. This equates to $1.1 million per tax payer. A *Washington Post* blog cites it closer to $30 trillion. Either way these are mind-numbing statistics to consider, and they imply greater future issues are at hand, but for the purpose of our discussion, and to keep things more manageable, we will only address the "current" $17 trillion figure. **Unfunded liabilities:** *http://www.forbes.com/sites/realspin/2014/01/17/you-think-the-deficit-is-bad-federal-unfunded-liabilities-exceed-127-trillion/*

http://www.washingtonpost.com/blogs/fact-checker/wp/2013/10/23/does-the-united-states-have-128-trillion-in-unfunded-liabilities/

The government debt should be a concern to every American, especially for the next generations (and not by choice). If we think we can attempt to solve our debt issues, the first step may actually be to familiarize ourselves with our deficit issues. The deficit is synonymous with negative cash flow, and this is pertinent because debt (the payments on) requires cash flow.

Concept 2: Deficit

How much is the government taking in versus spending. There is an important analogy with your household's financial situation. You should compare how much you earn each year to how much you spend. Is there money left over? If there is, then you are running a surplus. If there isn't money left over, and spending exceeds income, you are running a deficit. Using 2013 numbers from the Office of Management and Budget, we can see that the United States currently takes in approximately $2.82 trillion in tax revenues, and it spends approximately $3.5 trillion ($680 billion deficit) making up the difference through borrowing. Therefore, the government is not only running a large deficit, it also possesses a debt-to-income ratio of nearly six to one, or $17 trillion to $2.82 trillion.

http://money.cnn.com/2013/10/30/news/economy/deficit-2013-treasury/

This is analogous to your household earning $100,000, spending $124,000, and having nearly $600,000 in debt. Is that a healthy financial situation?

A family that earns $100,000 but spends $124,000 knows that it can only continue to float an additional $24,000 per year for so long. Either that family needs to increase its income or drastically cut down on its spending.

Given the government's debt levels and spending habits, what are the potential solutions?

Concept 3: QE, Quantitative Easing (labeled by some as money printing)

Given our government's debt and deficit situation, we have three viable resolutions to entertain. Rob Arnott, the chairman of Research Affiliates and the manager of the PIMCO All Asset (and All Asset and All Authority) Fund, explained these solutions best. In his Q&A session for the August 2012 Pimco Views Paper, Arnott explained, "As our debt level soars, we must eventually address it by following one of three paths: austerity, abrogation, or reflation. Access to a printing press gives a nation the option of monetizing the debt by debasing the currency. This, of course, is the path of least political resistance, because political leaders simply cannot deflect the blame when they choose austerity or default."

In other words, we have three potential resolutions to our financial quandary. This predicament is no different than what a household in a similar situation would face. One, we could take our medicine, make massive cuts in our spending, and increase taxes, thereby creating a surplus that would allow us to more easily pay down our debt. This option is politically difficult and unpopular. Two, we could default on our debt (see first solution). Three, we could print money and devalue the dollar. In theory, this would make the debt easier to pay down. It would make the debt more manageable, as you pay back debt with cheaper dollars. Ultimately, all three potentials are on the table, but for our purposes I want to further explore the third option because I assume that most Americans have never entertained that as a viable solution that could (or would) be considered. In addition, the easiest political track quite often is the path chosen.

Inflation may not be favorable when you are purchasing a gallon of milk or a tank of gas, but it makes it easier to pay down debt. As inflation kicks in, everything in theory gets more expensive, or it takes more dollars to purchase things, as the dollars are worth less. Everything requires more dollars at this point, except for your debt. Your mortgage or car loan payment that you locked in at a low fixed rate doesn't inflate. It stays at that same dollar figure and required payment. As more easy money comes into your household, bread and eggs cost more, but you now have more dollars. This makes it easier for you to pay off your fixed debt, which hasn't been inflating. Again, you are essentially paying off debt with cheaper dollars than what you originally borrowed.

A good follow-up article to read online is the following *Forbes* article, which states that the goal is to devalue the dollar: http://www.forbes.com/sites/charleskadlec/2012/02/06/the-federal-reserves-explicit-goal-devalue-the-dollar-33/.

Even the International Monetary Fund (providing some global perspective) in their white paper *Public Debt Dynamics: The Effects of Austerity, Inflation, and Growth Shocks* by Reda Cherif and Fuad Hasanov acknowledge the interrelationship of inflationary policies and debt. "Looser monetary policy with less aggressive interest rate hikes may be needed for the inflation shock to play a strong role in reducing debt. For instance, Krugman (1998, 2011), Mankiw (2009), and Rogoff (2009, 2011) have argued for a higher inflation target that the Fed would announce in the times of the zero-interest bound to improve economic recovery and speed up the deleveraging process."

> The International Monetary Fund (IMF) promotes international financial stability and monetary cooperation. It also seeks to facilitate international trade, promote high employment and sustainable economic growth, and reduce poverty around the world. Created in 1945, the IMF is governed by and accountable to the 188 countries that make up its near-global membership. (Source: http://www.imf.org/external/np/exr/facts/glance.htm)

Would our government and the Federal Reserve really want inflation? Perhaps we can best answer that by emphasizing what the Fed desperately doesn't want. The opposite of inflation is deflation. With deflation, the prices of goods and incomes decline, and the system contracts. As income declines, it becomes more difficult to pay down debts with fixed payments. A contracting economy isn't beneficial to most Americans, especially those households, businesses, and governments carrying excessive debt.

The Fed has expressed a high level of confidence that it has the tools to help us avoid such an environment. Bernanke, the former Fed chief, is perhaps most famous for his deflation-fighting nickname, Helicopter Ben. On November 21, 2002, he gave a somewhat famous speech before the National Economists Club in Washington, DC.

This speech can be found here: http://www.federalreserve.gov/BOARDDOCS/SPEECHES/2002/20021121/default.htm.

In that speech, Bernanke said, "The sources of deflation are not a mystery. Deflation is in almost all cases a side effect of a collapse of aggregate demand—a drop in spending so severe that producers must cut prices on an ongoing basis in order to find buyers. Likewise, the economic effects of a deflationary episode, for the most part, are similar to those of any other sharp decline in aggregate spending—namely, recession, rising unemployment, and financial stress. If we do fall into deflation, however, **we can take comfort that the logic of the printing press example must assert itself, and sufficient injections of money will ultimately always reverse a deflation**."

He remarked that the government can almost certainly avoid deflation by printing more dollars. He referred to a statement that Milton Friedman, a Nobel Prize-winning economist, made about using a helicopter drop of money to fight deflation. Ever since then, Bernanke has had the nickname Helicopter Ben.

Bernanke concluded his speech by saying, **"Sustained deflation can be highly destructive to a modern economy and should be strongly resisted. I hope to have persuaded you that the Federal Reserve and other economic policymakers would be far from helpless in the face of deflation, even should the federal funds rate hit its zero bound."**

In hindsight, that is about where we sit today.

Bernanke argues that the Fed is prepared to do whatever it takes to prevent deflation, and according to the *Wall Street Journal*, his successor, Janet Yellen, is from the same school of thought. Notably, a *Wall Street Journal* poll indicated that economists do not see much difference between Bernanke and his successor, Yellen, in terms of policy. While chairmen have changed, it appears philosophy will not (http://blogs.wsj.com/economics/2013/10/09/economists-dont-see-much-difference-between-yellen-fed-and-third-bernanke-term/).

Of the three previous outlined debt solutions, the probability of inflation playing a significant role cannot be ignored. This is especially true given the nature of the Fed's recent monetary policies, known as quantitative easing.

Quantitative Easing: "An unconventional monetary policy in which a central bank purchases government securities or other securities from the market in order to lower interest rates and increase the money supply. Quantitative easing increases the money supply by flooding financial institutions with capital in an effort to promote increased lending and liquidity." (Source: Investopedia)

For a visual explanation animated on a whiteboard, consider visiting: http://www.marketplace.org/topics/business/whiteboard/quantitative-easing

For those reading this on the Kindle with Internet access, I had to include this next link. If you are reading this in hard copy, forgive my usage of a link to a video clip. However, I do recommend that you watch this video when you have the chance.

You may be asking yourself, "Can the Fed just print more money? Is that possible? Is that something that they would seriously consider?" To hear it straight from the horse's mouth, and for some good laughs, consider viewing this little segment that aired on *The Daily Show*: **www.thedailyshow.com/watch/tue-december-7-2010/the-big-bank-theory**

The video first shows Bernanke on *60 Minutes* saying that the Fed doesn't print money. In actuality, it is buying government bonds and mortgage-backed securities, but it is doing so with digital currency rather than paper money. The clip then shows a previous *60 Minutes* interview in which Bernanke admits to their quantitative easing programs as "being akin to printing money." *The Daily Show* edited the clips in a fashion that is quite humorous, as it shows the same person discussing the same subject but making two somewhat contradictory statements. I cannot do it justice, but for a good laugh on this topic, this video is definitely worth watching.

At the time of this writing the Federal Reserve has already initiated several rounds of quantitative easing programs. In addition to keeping the federal funds interest rate at the lowest levels in our lifetimes, the Fed has been purchasing billions of dollars per month of treasuries and mortgage-backed securities (range of purchases at the time of this writing has been between $45 and $85 billion per month), which (at the higher level) equates to just under $1 trillion ($900,000,000,000) per year. And where do they get the money to do this? Going back to the *Daily Show* clip, with a few key strokes they create the money to then buy the government's debt. Or in Jon Stewart's interpretation, *the Fed has been printing money to buy government debt.*

Again, I ask you, is this "normal"? Or perhaps, this time around, things are actually different?

> As defined by the SEC, "**Mortgage-backed securities (MBS)** are debt obligations that represent claims to the cash flows from pools of mortgage loans, most commonly on residential property. Mortgage loans are purchased from banks, mortgage companies, and other originators and then assembled into pools by a governmental, quasi-governmental, or private entity. The entity then issues securities that represent claims on the principal and interest payments made by borrowers on the loans in the pool, a process known as securitization. Most MBSs are issued by the Government National Mortgage Association (Ginnie Mae), a US government agency, or the Federal National Mortgage Association (Fannie Mae) and the Federal Home Loan Mortgage Corporation (Freddie Mac), US government-sponsored enterprises."

In other words, the United States issues bonds (akin to taking out loans) and pays interest on those bonds (loans). The benefit of issuing a bond or taking out a loan is that the government (just like a family) can now use the proceeds to help fund their current spending. However, there needs to be a buyer of the bond (or lender) who is willing to give money today in return for those interest payments. This is similar to a bank agreeing to provide a family with a mortgage. In a free market system, in order to attract a buyer or someone who would lend money to the United States now, they (in theory) have to offer an attractive interest rate on the bond.

Think of it this way: if they were offering 0 percent on their bonds (in a free market) how many people would show up to purchase them? Probably none. What if the United States was offering 15 percent interest payments to those who would loan them the money (purchase the new bonds)? The line would be long. Again, in a free market with competition, equilibrium points are typically reached.

However, through quantitative easing, the Fed has stepped in as the primary buyer of bonds issued by the United States. Acting as the market, by doing all of their purchasing and being price agnostic, they are helping to keep rates low. Without the Fed instituting this program and allowing free markets to determine the interest rate, the United States would most likely have to offer higher interest rates on its debt.

Higher rates mean additional cash flow or deficit problems for the United States, as higher payments are required on debt. Additionally, higher interest rates on home loans have a major impact on US real estate, which often makes up a major portion of the net worth of most families. As you can see, QE has a dramatic impact on many markets, and the Fed is being as aggressive as it ever has.

Continuing our comparison to our American family, who is earning $100,000 per year, spending $124,000 per year, and carrying $600,000 of debt. Even though their financial situation isn't strong or stable, they are able to continue to get more and more lines of credit to help them continue to fund their lifestyle, until they cannot and have to turn to less conventional means to secure additional loans. It turns out that Uncle Joe (a relative, but not especially close to the family) is a loan shark and is more than happy to provide the family with ongoing funds at very low interest as a favor. So no longer is the family utilizing the free market, or "normal," banking outlets to obtain further lines of credit; they have actually begun working with a relative who they view as their lender of last resort.

A few years go by, and the family is thrilled that Uncle Joe continues to support them. But they do become concerned with the amount of debt they have with a family member as it makes them feel somewhat uncomfortable. In addition, they are also worried about Joe's financial stability and whether he can continue to provide them with cheap credit. One night at a holiday party, the family tiptoed into the conversation with Joe. Thankfully he reassured them that there is nothing to worry about. However, he was also, unexpectedly, very short with them and told them not to ever bring up the subject again. Joe emphasized the fact that nobody needed to know how he made his money or how he managed his finances. "Consider me a black box," said Joe, "and just be happy to continue to live your lifestyle."

The analogy here is that the Fed stepping in as the lender of last resort is unusual, as is the fact that they have quadrupled their balance sheet since 2008, as is the fact that they are holding interest rates artificially low, and as is the fact that all of their financial activities are not 100 percent transparent.

Where are these policies and this situation leading us? As the saying goes, history repeats itself. However, we have never seen this before (which is why I argue this time is different). The massive quantitative easing policy is labeled by many, including Warren Buffett, as a "huge experiment." That is not very reassuring. "QE is like watching a good movie, because I don't know how it will end," says Buffett. "Anyone who owns stocks will reevaluate his hand when it happens, and that will happen very quickly."

http://finance.fortune.cnn.com/2013/05/04/buffett-worries-about-feds-huge-experiment/

Two potential outcomes of these policies could very well be 1) speculation, and 2) inflation.

Speculation

Investment speculation may be amplified through the use of cheap credit. If interest rates are low and it is inexpensive to borrow, many aggressive speculators will be inclined to borrow and invest with the lent money. One example of this can be seen through use of margin debt, money borrowed from a brokerage firm within an investment account. The following graph shows how margin debt levels have fluctuated throughout the years in conjunction with the rising and falling stock market. Again, it epitomizes emotional investing because investors are most willing to be aggressive (by borrowing to invest) when markets have had big run-ups (and are expensive) and least likely when markets are down (and cheap). As the graph demonstrates, when you have cheap credit and a rising market (viewed by speculators as an opportunity for higher returns) you will find accelerated speculation. The chart indicates that we are at highly elevated, borderline extreme, levels of margin debt in 2014.

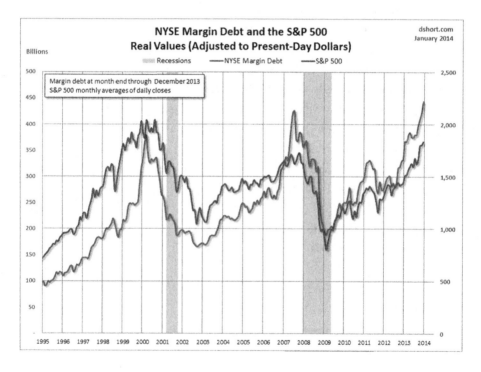

(Source: Advisor Perspectives, www.advisorperspectives.com, www.dshort.com)

Not only on a personal level, but at a corporate level, 2013 witnessed some of the largest company share repurchase programs (when companies buy their own stock) ever seen. How were these companies financing the purchases of their own stock? Well, according to Bloomberg, a good amount was from borrowing (issuing bonds) facilitated by a low interest rate environment. "Apple Inc. to Walt Disney Co. and International Business Machines Corp. (IBM) took advantage of record low interest rates to raise an unprecedented amount of debt financing and repurchased stock, helping boost per-share U.S. earnings for four years." (Source: Bloomberg)

http://www.bloomberg.com/news/print/2013-12-16/apple-to-ibm-push-buyback-to-record-trading-as-volume-slows-1-.html

Borrowed money is flowing into the stock market and pushing up prices. Speculation often leads to bubbles, which promotes more volatility (massive swings up and down) ahead. As I mentioned in the beginning of this chapter, hopefully this information can further motivate you to entertain the proactive investment strategies outlined in later chapters as opposed to just passive buy-and-hold.

These are just two examples of speculation, but as David Stockman, former budget director under President Reagan, wrote in a critical *New York Times* op-ed piece, this activity is mirrored in even bigger markets with even bigger players. "...the Fed, which dropped interest rates to zero and then digitally printed new money at the astounding rate of $600 million per hour. Fast-money speculators have been 'purchasing' giant piles of Treasury debt and mortgage-backed securities, almost entirely by using short-term overnight money borrowed at essentially zero cost, thanks to the Fed...If and when the Fed even hints at shrinking its balance sheet, it will elicit a tidal wave of sell orders, because even a modest drop in bond prices would destroy the arbitrageurs' profits."

http://www.nytimes.com/2013/03/31/opinion/sunday/sundown-in-america.html?_r=0

Inflation

Another potential outcome of these policies is that easy money often creates inflationary environments. However, with all this talk of printing money, one would assume we would already be seeing elevated levels of inflation, but where is it? In theory, if the Fed injects money (in the form of increased bank reserves), this should create credit, which would stimulate growth. This would then create jobs, which would lead to low unemployment. This would then lead to wage growth and eventually inflation. As we examine this further, we see that there is a blockage—purposely or not—in the flow of this formula.

The money supply is made up of the monetary base, M1, and M2. The monetary base, as shown in the next slide, is the sum of the currency in circulation and the reserve balances, which are deposits that banks hold at the Federal Reserve. We will discuss this further in a moment. M1 is the sum of the currency that the public holds and transaction deposits at banking institutions. M2 is M1 plus savings deposits and money market funds. Notice the gradual incline over time that abruptly increases (almost four-fold) since 2008. Rhetorical question: which parts of the graph seem "normal" to you and which parts don't?

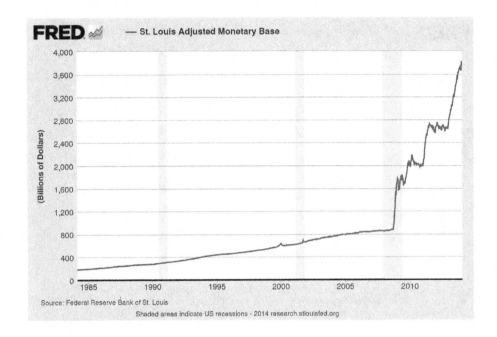

Data Source: FRED, Federal Reserve Economic Data, Federal Reserve Bank of St. Louis: *Adjusted Monetary Base [BASE]*; Federal Reserve Bank of St. Louis; http://research.stlouisfed.org/fred2/series/BASE; accessed February 19, 2014.

The distinction between these different categories on money is important because it helps us better explain and comprehend where all of the quantitative easing dollars went. They did not go into the local economy, where massive amounts of currency would most likely be inflationary. Instead (this is the key), the Federal Reserve is holding a lion's share on reserve for banks. What is going on here, and what does this mean? Notice the high correlation between the monetary base graph and the excess reserves of depository institutions on the subsequent chart.

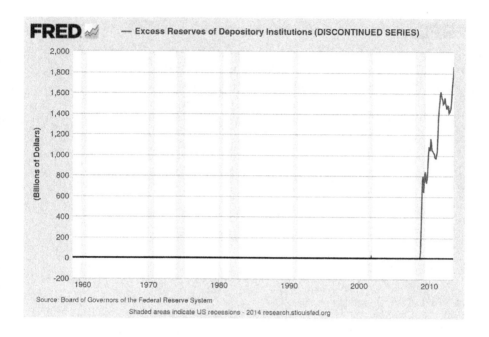

Data Source: FRED, Federal Reserve Economic Data, Federal Reserve Bank of St. Louis: *Excess Reserves of Depository Institutions [EXCRESNS]*; Board of Governors of the Federal Reserve System; http://research.stlouisfed.org/fred2/series/EXCRESNS; accessed February 19, 2014.

The US economics editor for the *Economist*, Greg Ip, perhaps explains this best. With massive stimulus, you would assume that we would be witnessing elevated levels of inflation already. In his book *The Little Book of Economics*, he points out, "The second unknown (after the Fed's political risk of policies) is whether printing all that money will create inflation. Monetarists who see a tight link between all those extra reserves and inflation certainly think so. But they're probably wrong. That's because… reserves can't cause inflation if they aren't lent and spent." He goes on to say, "Luckily, in 2008 the Fed got a new tool to work with: the right to pay interest on excess reserves (IOER). If IOER is 2 percent, banks will keep those reserves at the Fed rather than lend them at less than 2 percent in the Fed Funds market."

Essentially, the banks are holding most of the freely created money on the sidelines. The banks are holding these excess reserves with the Fed, from whom they are receiving risk-free interest payments. Therefore, this may actually dissuade banks from lending and thus keep inflation at bay for the moment.

Stockman, in his op-ed, also noted, "By default, the Fed has resorted to a radical, unchartered spree of money printing. But the flood of liquidity, instead of spurring banks to lend and corporations to spend, has stayed trapped in the canyons of Wall Street, where it is inflating yet another unsustainable bubble."

In summary, we aren't seeing inflation yet due in large part to the fact that banks have not been lending. This is partly due to the hangover from the prior lending binge (risk adverse), increased underwriting scrutiny, and tighter regulations. However, the Fed is also (perhaps most importantly) rewarding the banks with risk-free interest payments. If these policies ever change—they often do—then the landscape for inflation may change drastically as well. **The gun is loaded but the trigger hasn't been pulled just yet.** Hence many smart observers think that these reserves being released into our local economies may be on the horizon.

In an interview with Charles Plosser of Philadelphia in the February 2013 issue of *Money* magazine, the author noted, "The Fed has poured huge amounts of money into banks' reserves. Right now a lot of that money is just sitting there; Plosser's worry is that the money could eventually pour too fast into the real economy, fueling inflation if the Fed doesn't act." In other words, the potential for inflation is very much present. However, this hasn't materialized yet. If it does happen, the Fed wants to make sure it is controlled rather than runaway hyperinflation. One way they can help control such events from occurring would be through raising the rates.

It conceptually makes sense that it is imperative to avoid deflation (contracting economy) and favor inflationary measures to handle massive debts and large deficits. Currently the most powerful institution that affects markets, the Fed, supports this view. In addition, for the longest time all we have seen is long-term inflation. Is it possible that the Fed loses control over black swan free market forces and deflation dominates? I suppose it is possible. However, if the Fed has anything to say about it, they will use all of their resources and firepower to combat such an environment. Therefore, I recommend playing the percentages and start to assemble an arsenal of inflation hedges (see the next chapter) for the future.

> Definition of black swan: "An event or occurrence that deviates beyond what is normally expected of a situation and that would be extremely difficult to predict. Nassim Nicholas Taleb, a finance professor and former Wall Street trader, popularized this term."
> —*Investopedia*

Although the odds of future inflation are highly probable, they are not guaranteed. The same may not be said for the next topic.

Concept 4: Rising Rates

Interest rate levels affect the amount of interest on loans and savings accounts. According to this theory, when the interest on a loan is low, it is easy to become profitable from a company's standpoint. Cheap money can be put to use, which is stimulative. In addition, when the interest on savings accounts is lower, riskier assets like stocks and bonds become more attractive, and there is less of an incentive to keep money in savings (but be careful of the reverse).

Each month, the Federal Reserve, through its Federal Open Market Committee (FOMC), targets a specific level for the federal funds rate.

This rate directly influences other short-term interest rates. It immediately impacts LIBOR, which is the interest rate that banks charge each other for one-month, three-month, six-month, and one-year loans. It also impacts the prime rate, which is the rate that banks charge their best customers. In this way, the federal funds rate also affects interest rates that are paid on deposits, bank loans, credit cards, and adjustable-rate mortgages. Longer-term interest rates are also indirectly influenced. Usually investors want a higher rate for a longer-term treasury note, as they want to be paid more in return for making a longer-term commitment. The yields on treasury notes drive long-term conventional mortgage interest rates.

Therefore, you can see how much the economy and financial system hinges on what the Fed decides regarding rates. From a very high level, if they want to stimulate the economy they lower rates, making credit more easily obtainable. If they want to prevent runaway inflation or cool down an overheated economy, they might consider raising rates.

Right now, the Fed is holding rates down in two ways. It is keeping short-term rates near zero by targeting the federal funds rate, which is the rate at which banks lend money to one another overnight. And it is holding down long-term rates through the monthly purchases of treasuries (via QE as previously outlined).

Let's take a closer look at the next graph, which is a historical chart of the federal funds rate. When you see the spike in the middle of the graph, many of you will recall the late 1970s and early 1980s. Mortgage and CD (certificates of deposit) were way above what they are today. Quickly follow the graph down with your eyes and see where we stand at this point in time. We are at nearly zero and historically lower than we have ever been.

Rhetorical question: Where do you think we most likely will go from here?

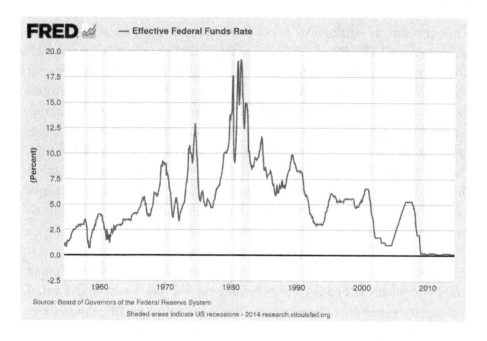

Data Source: FRED, Federal Reserve Economic Data, Federal Reserve Bank of St. Louis: *Effective Federal Funds Rate [FEDFUNDS]*; Board of Governors of the Federal Reserve System; http://research.stlouisfed.org/fred2/series/FEDFUNDS; accessed February 19, 2014.

I recommend that you pay attention to rate policies because they will have a major impact on the economy and your portfolio—most notably bonds.

How do rising rates impact bond values?

Imagine that you have purchased a $1,000 bond that is paying 3 percent interest. What if rates begin to rise? What if new CDs are paying 4 percent and new bonds are paying 5 percent? If you wanted to sell your 3-percent interest bond, what type of price would you get? Why would an investor choose to buy your bond when better options are available? They wouldn't do so unless you gave them a worthy discount. As higher—and often safer—interest-bearing options come onto the market, the value of lower-interest-bearing or equal but riskier (credit-risk) options is less appealing. The value to potential buyers must go down. This is the reason that bond prices will fall. In summary, rising rates often lead to falling bond prices and represent an inverse correlation.

Because of decades of strong bond performance, conservative investors are very comfortable with this asset class. However, let's not forget the Gretzky quote from the introduction: "Skate to where the puck is going to be, not where it has been." Where are rates going from here?

Interestingly enough, you can quickly glance at the previous graph and pinpoint the catalyst that instigated the great three-decade-long bull market in US bonds: falling rates. Ever since 1981, rates have fallen and bonds have rallied.

You may agree with me that this should be a major concern to the majority of bond investors (often conservative, income-seeking retirees). Although this information doesn't make headlines in your local paper or the six o'clock news, there hasn't been a total blackout of cautionary warnings. For example, the Financial Industry Regulatory Authority (FINRA) is the largest independent regulator for all securities firms doing business in the United States. It released an advisory notice to investors about the risks of holding bonds in rising rate environments: http://www.finra.org/Investors/ProtectYourself/InvestorAlerts/Bonds/P204318.

In the October 30, 2010, Barrons article "Good-bye, Great Bond Bull Market," Pimco's Bill Gross addressed the current Fed actions and the bond market environment. As the "Bond King" said, "Check writing in the trillions is not a bondholder's friend… It is, in fact, inflationary, and if truth be told, somewhat of a Ponzi scheme." The article goes on to say, "Say good-bye, then, to the great thirty-year bull market in bonds."

Again, interest rates are at their lowest levels, and at some point in the future interest rates will begin to climb back up again. This may be bad news for bonds (i.e., declining prices). Moreover, rising rates may also require the United States to pay higher interest rates on its debt, further impacting deficit (cash flow) issues.

So, here is my concern: The baby boomer generation is in retirement or close to entering retirement. They will want to reduce the risk exposure—or at least think they are reducing the risk—of their portfolios. At the same time, they are looking for income-producing assets. What do you think they are going to invest in? Conventional wisdom says that it will be bonds!

This is problematic because investors who held the traditional sixty–forty (60 percent stocks and 40 percent bonds) before retirement will likely be considering reducing risk—or so they think. The majority of the money will be invested in an asset class that has served them well, but moving forward may have some significant headwinds (rising rates) confronting them.

Three Key Take-Aways:

1. The Fed is dead set against deflation. For reasons outlined above, it will attempt to target moderate inflation over time. Therefore, we need to have inflation hedges in our portfolios.
2. Whether it is due to inflation or other market forces, interest rates have nowhere to go but up. This tends to lead to declining bond values. Therefore, we need to prudently adjust and manage away from the interest-rate-sensitive fixed-income (bond) exposures in our portfolios.
3. Very low interest rates and easy money policies can encourage speculation, which may lead to additional bubbles and volatility in the markets. Stock investors may want to implement strategies that will help reduce portfolio volatility and/or tactical strategies that may allow them to sidestep the next decline.

> **In summary**
>
> - Current US debt and deficit measures are very high.
> - To alleviate such issues and to stimulate the economy, the Fed has adopted its most aggressive policies since its inception.
> - There are no guarantees. There are only playing percentages. However, such measures point to speculation, eventual inflation, and rising interest rates.

I can only say: I'm sorry, America. As a former Federal Reserve official, I was responsible for executing the centerpiece program of the Fed's first plunge into the bond-buying experiment known as quantitative easing. The central bank continues to spin QE as a tool for helping Main Street. But I've come to recognize the program for what it really is: the greatest backdoor Wall Street bailout of all time.

—Andrew Huszar, November 11, 2013

CHAPTER 5

STOCKS, BONDS, CASH, AND THE TRAGIC 401(K) HANDCUFF

Question: Do you think your 401(k) offers a good variety of investment options?

Before we move forward, let's examine where our conventional asset classes (stocks, bonds, and cash) stand at this juncture. Working in reverse order, **cash** is not attractive as an asset class for reasonable appreciation potential. With interest rates at historical lows, we are unable at the moment to obtain reasonable returns on savings, money market, or certificates of deposit accounts. Eliminating cash as a viable option leaves us with two remaining asset classes to consider from the Old World menu of asset classes: stocks and bonds. These are the two components of the traditional sixty–forty balanced portfolio.

As we examined already in the last chapter, **bond** values will decrease when—not if—interest rates begin to increase (reverse correlation). Therefore, the vast majority of bond mutual fund and ETFs will decline in value as interest rates eventually elevate off of the bottom basement levels that they currently are at. Eliminating cash and the vast majority of bond funds as viable options leaves us with one asset class to consider from the Old World menu of asset classes: stocks.

> **Caution:** Conservative investors (i.e., senior citizens) do not have an appetite for risky investments, yet they don't have ideal options to choose from. Cash pays close to nothing, and bonds, which are often synonymous with conservative investing, now carry risk of declining values.

By using the process of elimination in our classic asset classes, we are left with one favorable option: **stocks**. This is where the story gets exciting in good and bad ways.

- As cash investors realize that they earn nothing and that they lose their purchasing power to inflation when they keep their money in cash, won't most of these investors look elsewhere for return?
- As bond investors realize the value of their bonds performing in a manner that is uncharacteristic compared to what they have been used to for the past three decades, won't most of these investors look elsewhere for return?
- As an increasing number of investors realize that stocks may be the only place to offer growth opportunities, doesn't this set us all up for a major bull market?

Well, potentially yes, yes, and yes. Investors may have little choice but to put their money into stocks. As a result, we may actually witness the opposite of a meltdown in the markets: a melt-up!

Normally, this would be very exciting news. You might say, "Of course it is good news. How can it not be good news?" This would be fantastic news if stocks were selling at deep discounts with huge room to run for the next decade. Well, what if I told you that stocks are historically not cheap. In fact, they can be considered to be expensive. Unfortunately, they are selling at a premium. If history is the only guide we have, the odds of a decade-long super bull run are not in our favor. This is not impossible, but the odds are not in our favor.

One technical term to become familiar with is price-to-earnings ratio, which is more commonly called PE ratio. PE ratio refers to the price of a company compared to the earnings that it generates. More specifically, the PE ratio is the current price of the stock divided by the company's earnings per share. We can calculate this not only for a specific company but also for markets in general, such as the S&P 500 or the Dow Jones Industrial Average. This allows us to take the temperature of the market as a whole.

The following is not a perfect analogy, but it resonates well with most people. You can think of the PE ratio in terms of a home. This is a familiar example that is easy to visualize. Imagine that your neighbor's house is going up for sale. Since you know the neighborhood and the relative values of the various properties in the area, you know what is an expensive or a cheap price for this house. Let's assume that you think that the house should sell for $500,000. Let's also assume that you have $500,000 that you just inherited in cash; as outlined above, it is earning nothing. Let's assume you are considering buying the property and renting it out. In this case, the rental income can be considered profit for the purposes of our analogy. If you think you could collect $3,000 per month in rent, this would equate to $36,000 over the course of the year. For the purposes of our rough analogy, $500,000 divided by $36,000 would equate to a PE ratio of 13.89.

What if the house, to your surprise, listed at $250,000? Since you know the real estate in the area like the back of your hand, and you are quite sure that you could secure a renter for $3,000 per month, this sounds like a pretty good deal. In this case, your PE ratio would be 6.94 ($250,000 divided by $36,000). This would result in a lower PE ratio. This is a cheaper transaction, better for you, the investor.

Conversely, what if the house surprisingly listed at $1 million? You would be fairly certain that you could only collect $3,000 per month in rental income. The list price of your neighbor's old house would seem expensive for your investment. This would result in a PE ratio of 27.78. One million dollars divided by $36,000 equals a more expensive transaction and much less appeal to you, the investor.

High PE ratios may not always signify poor prospects for investment. Some investors may be willing to pay higher prices for a cutting-edge technology firm that boasts tremendous promise for future innovation and profits (e.g., Amazon.com). However, promise, innovation potential, and profits are much different for one company than for a broad index of hundreds of companies in all different sectors. What analyzing the PE ratio of an entire index like the S&P 500 does provide us with is a clear gauge of its level of expensiveness and cheapness of stocks as an asset class.

In our neighbor's real estate example, since we were estimating what we think our profits would be in the future year, we used what is called a forward PE ratio. This is one of the three most commonly referred to variations of the PE. In addition, there is also the current PE and the Shiller PE. Current PE looks at reported earnings from the past year, while the Shiller PE takes a longer time horizon and is based on the average inflation-adjusted earnings from the previous ten years. It is named after Robert J. Shiller, the Nobel Prize-winning professor at Yale University. Without getting too technical, it is also known as the cyclically adjusted price-to-earnings ratio (CAPE), as it looks back over a longer time horizon and various market cycles. Technical information aside, this ratio has had an uncanny ability to signal when markets become expensive and when they are cheap. Keep in mind that investors have a herd mentality, and they can thus continue to run expensive prices higher or discount prices lower. Therefore, this isn't a precise timing mechanism, rather a general gauge that provides us with a temperature check on the market.

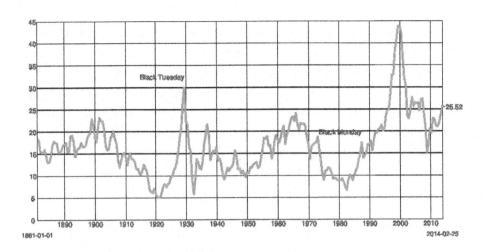

Current Shiller PE Ratio: 25.52

Mean: 16.52

Median: 15.91

Min: 4.78 (Dec 1920)

Max: 44.20 (Dec 1999)

Above is the Shiller PE ratio (as of February 25, 2014) courtesy of: http://www.multpl.com/shiller-pe/.

The $64,000 question is: What is the temperature of the market? Is it cheap, expensive, or somewhere in between?

The historically average Shiller PE is 16.52, and at the time of this writing we are above 25. This has only been eclipsed three other times previous. It was eclipsed in 1929, which led to the Great Depression, and it was eclipsed in 1999, which led to the tech bubble burst. It was also eclipsed in the middle of the 2000s, which led to the collapse of 2008.

I suppose that by process of elimination, **stocks** should be an asset class to consider. After all, they can always run higher, as we witnessed in the late nineties. Since cash and bonds are not very appealing, investment dollars have to find a home somewhere, and therefore may be further funneled into the market. **However, if you are planning on buying and holding, know that you are not getting in at the ground floor. The Shiller PE indicates that stocks are not cheap.** Therefore, if you plan on maintaining stock exposure, it is important to heighten your awareness around defensive strategies and/or exit strategies for stocks.

At some point within the next five years, it will no longer be prudent to implement buy-and-hold. In addition, it will be important to expand your awareness about other asset classes and management techniques that exist beyond buying and holding stocks, bonds, and cash.

The 401(k) Handcuff

In light of the stocks, bonds, and cash discussion in conjunction with the effect of rising rates from the previous chapter, I want to outline an unfortunate impediment to your financial success in future years. It has to do with the limited investment options provided by most work-based retirement plans—401(k), 403(b), etc.—and, more specifically, the inherent flaws embedded within the increasingly popular target date retirement funds. These limited options plus the current environment equals the 401(k) handcuff, and most people have no idea it even exists.

A very common list mutual fund offering within 401(k) retirement plans resembles something like this list below (which happens to be a real-life example):

1 Stable Value (Cash Alternative)

3 Bond Funds

1 Balanced (Stocks and Bonds)

8 Stock Funds

- 3 Large Cap
- 2 International
- 1 Mid Cap
- 1 Small Cap
- 1 Total Market (Large, Mid, and Small)

12 Target Date Funds

In reviewing these options, at first glance, average investors may conclude that the list is comprehensive. In addition, they might also assume that their employer performed a high level of due diligence and would only provide a plan that passed a rigorous examination.

On second thought, in light of our previous discussions, let's examine these offerings more carefully:

The *stable value* fund offers little value, especially in this low-rate environment. The *bond options* are not appealing either if we are close to heading into a rising-rate environment. As we will analyze in the next chapter, there are some particular types of bonds that may be beneficial to hold, but these are very type specific and typically not represented in the limited options provided. The *balanced fund* is similar to the classic sixty–forty portfolio that historically has suited many investors, but as this book outlines in great detail, it may not be as efficient moving forward.

The true deception is in the offering of the eight different *stock funds*. Most would conclude that this offers plenty of diversification. However, as we outlined with the correlation matrix, all those funds will move predominantly in unison together. Therefore, within stocks there will be no defensive mechanisms to protect the employee's balance from the next major decline (as perceived diversification won't). This leaves us with the most prominent types of offerings within the plan, which are the *target date funds*. Although they may appear to be tailored to your specific retirement goals, by listing your retirement date in the name of the strategy, I encourage you to reevaluate whether they are the best option for your savings.

Target Date Funds, Looking Under the Hood

Now that we have reviewed the potential dangers that a rising rate environment has on bonds, I can better explain my concern with target date retirement funds. The graph below is an example of how this company's target date funds shift from stocks (equities) to bonds (short term and fixed income) over time. You will notice immediately that before and after "RET," the retirement date, exposure levels to bonds increases.

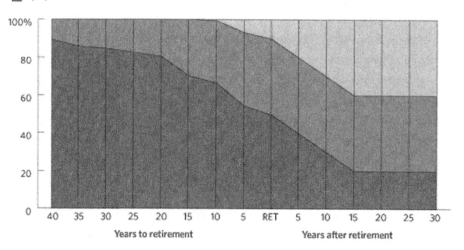

Source: http://www.ici.org/faqs/faq/faqs_target_date

My issues with this strategy:

Issue 1: As we outlined in chapter three, the entire portfolio manages risk based on time. No consideration is given to the individual investor's unique personal risk tolerance.

Issue 2: Again, because it manages the asset allocation based only on time, this strategy does not factor in the current market environment. Knowing what you know now about rising rates and how they impact bond prices, this strategy warrants a rhetorical question. How would you feel if your target date fund began shifting more heavily into fixed income as rates began to rise?

Issue 3: The target date funds will invest in a broad array of bond funds. However, as noted in the next chapter, there is a definite pecking order regarding the best bonds to own in an environment of rising rates. Unfortunately, these funds will not handpick specific bond types. Instead, they will typically own a big broad basket and will increase this exposure as time elapses, perhaps even in the midst of rising rates. Again, these strategies give little consideration for the current environment (historically low interest rates), at a time when specific bond-type selection will matter most.

Sadly, these strategies are very prevalent within the work-based retirement plan, which is often the family's largest investment account. The concept of target date retirement funds is excellent in theory. However, its lack of personalization and consideration for the current market environment is flawed and potentially risky for the unassuming investor.

What can you do to avoid the 401(k) handcuff?

Solution 1: Some employers are beginning to offer a do-it-yourself open architecture brokerage-linked option. This allows employees to manage their 401(k)s with a major brokerage house's platform, which offers thousands of options. This is often better than the restricted options of their current plan provider.

Solution 2: Ask your HR department for the summary plan description of the work-based retirement plan. Many companies allow for in-service withdrawals. This allows current employees to roll over their current 401(k) balance to an IRA, even before separation from service, and where they can invest on their own with a major brokerage firm.

Both of these options are becoming more popular, and they both allow for a work-around from the 401(k) handcuff.

At this point you may be throwing up your hands in frustration assuming that there is no good place to invest. What the following chapters will introduce you to will require you to expand your investment horizons and step outside the box of conventional solutions. As a little taste of what is to come, and to provide a light at the end of this tunnel, five solutions are worth consideration:

1) Type-specific investments
2) Alternative asset classes beyond the traditional stocks, bonds, and cash
3) Tactical asset management, proactively adjusting allocation percentages to various asset classes factoring in the current market environment
4) Trend analysis
5) Self-directed investment accounts

To reiterate, you probably won't find any of these options within your favorite savings accounts for retirement and college: 401(k)/403(b) retirement account and 529 college savings account!

The combination of interest rates near all-time lows and elevated stock valuations makes the investment environment for current retirees among the most challenging in history. Target date funds don't solve the problem and may actually compound it by shifting to a higher percentage of bonds at a time when future returns from bond funds are likely to be significantly lower than in the past.

—Ed Dempsey, CFP, CIO of Pension Partners

FIVE UNCONVENTIONAL SOLUTIONS

1. Type-Specific Investments

2. Alternative Asset Classes

3. Tactical Allocation Strategies

4. Trend Analysis

5. Self-Directed Investments

CHAPTER 6

SPECIFIC ASSET-CLASS SOLUTIONS TO INFLATION AND RISING RATES

Question: How do various asset classes perform in inflationary and rising interest rate environments?

*Note: Many of you will ask this question. This chapter gets very specific with the types of investments within asset classes (i.e., bonds) that may work best.

Inflation Solutions

In this chapter, we will spend less time on why we should consider inflation hedges and be conscious of rising rates, as this information was outlined in the previous chapter. Here we will get right to the point and discuss the type-specific asset classes to consider.

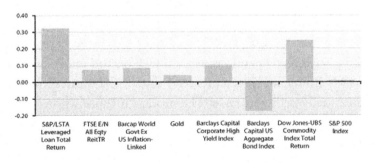

Period from Jan. 1, 1997 to Dec. 31, 2011 | Source: Gerstein Fisher research

http://www.forbes.com/sites/greggfisher/2012/03/05/hedging-inflation/

The above study reported in *Forbes* magazine looked at which asset classes had a positive correlation to inflation from 1997 through the end of 2011. As you can tell, most bonds (as represented by the broad bond index Barclays Capital US Aggregate Bond Index) don't perform well, even though this time frame was part of the thirty-year bull market for bonds. However, it is worth emphasizing that three unique types of bonds excelled in this environment (leverage loan, inflation linked, and high yield). Stock performance was somewhat indifferent, while a handful of less commonly held asset classes actually produced positive returns.

As investors, we need assets that help us navigate a number of diverse economic environments. The list below is not a list of current recommendations, but rather a list of tools in our toolbox that we can deploy if and when inflation appears.

1. Floating-Rate Bonds
2. Commodities
3. High-Yield Bonds
4. Treasury Inflation Protected Securities (TIPS)
5. Real Estate Investment Trusts (REITs)
6. Gold

As noted in chapter three, I am more concerned with you utilizing the right asset class than using the recommended funds listed here. Some people fall victim to analysis paralysis when they have too many choices. This can be overwhelming, and it can prevent some people from actually taking action, which defeats the purpose. Therefore, for those who would prefer to have some quality options, I have provided one to two mutual fund and ETF options for each recommended asset class.

Specific Asset-Class Solutions to Inflation and Rising Rates

*Note: These asset classes have shown resilience to inflationary environments in the past. Of course, previous results are no guarantee of future results. In utilizing these asset classes, a key determinant of your results will be the price that you buy them at. For example, as inflation increases, you might decide to add commodities to your portfolio. However, if they are overpriced and expensive, you might be disappointed with the results. Therefore, I recommend that you consider the valuation of the investment before you add that specific exposure to your portfolio.

1. **Floating-rate bonds:** Floating-rate loans are variable-rate loans made by financial institutions to companies that are generally considered to have low credit quality. They are also known as leveraged loans or senior bank loans. The loans are called "floating-rate" because the interest paid on the loans adjusts periodically—usually every thirty to ninety days—based on changes in widely accepted reference rates (e.g., LIBOR).

    Considerations for gaining exposure to floating-rate bonds:

Mutual Funds:	Eaton Vance Floating-Rate Adv (EABLX)
	Fidelity Floating-Rate High Income (FFRHX)
ETFs:	iShares Floating-Rate Note Fund (FLOT)
	SPDR Barclays Capital Investment Grade Floating-Rate (FLRN)

2. **Commodities:** Commodities are tangible assets, such as orange juice, wheat, cattle, gold, and oil.

    (We outline this asset class in greater detail in the next chapter.)

Considerations for gaining exposure to commodities:

Mutual Fund: Pimco Commodity Real Return Strategy (PCRDX)

ETF: Powershares DB Commodity Index Fund ETF (DBC)

3. **High-Yield Bonds:** These are high-paying bonds with lower credit ratings than investment-grade corporate bonds, treasury bonds, and municipal bonds. Because of the higher risk of default, these bonds pay a higher yield than investment-grade bonds. They are also known as "junk bonds."

Considerations for gaining exposure to high-yield bonds:

Mutual Funds: Fidelity High-Income (SPHIX)
Vanguard High-Yield Corporate Inv (VWEHX)

ETFs: iShares iBoxx $ HY Corp Bond Fund ETF (HYG)
SPDR Barclays Capital High-Yield Bond ETF (JNK)

4. **Treasury Inflation Protected Securities (TIPS):** This is a treasury security that is indexed to inflation to protect investors from its negative effects. TIPS are considered an extremely low-risk investment since the US government backs them and their par value rises with inflation, as measured by the consumer price index. Their interest rate remains fixed.

Considerations for gaining exposure to TIPS:

Mutual Funds: Pimco Real Return (PRRDX)
Vanguard Inflation Protected Securities Fund (VIPSX)

ETFs: iShares Barclays TIPS Bond Fund (TIP)
PIMCO Broad US TIPS Index Fund ETF (TIPZ)

5. **Real Estate Investment Trusts (REITs):** REITs combine the capital of many investors so that they can invest in various types of real estate. For example, they often invest in shopping malls, office buildings, apartments, warehouses, and hotels. REITs must pay distributions to its shareholders, and this amount must be equal to at least 90 percent of its taxable income.

   (We outline this asset class in greater detail in the next chapter.)

   Considerations for gaining exposure to REITs:

Mutual Funds:	T. Rowe Price Real Estate (TRREX)
	Vanguard REIT Index Inv (VGSIX)
ETFs:	SPDR Dow Jones REIT (RWR)
	Vanguard REIT Sector (VNQ)

6. **Gold:** This classification of metal is considered to be rare and/or have a high economic value. The higher relative values of gold are driven by various factors, including its rarity, its demand for jewelry, its desirability for investors seeking a safe haven, and its use as a currency alternative.

   (We outline this asset class in greater detail in the next chapter.)

   Considerations for gaining exposure to gold:

Mutual Funds:	Gold Bullion Strategy Investor (QGLDX)
ETFs:	iShares Gold Trust (IAU)
	SPDR Gold Shares (GLD)

Closed End Funds: Central Gold Trust (GTU)

A Broad Index of Stocks or Bonds

How will stocks and bonds perform in an inflationary environment? Elroy Dimson, Paul Marsh, and Mike Staunton of the London Business School produced an article in the 2012 *Credit Suisse Global Investment Returns Yearbook*. They found that during periods of marked inflation, equities (stocks) easily outperform bonds, which they found to be the worst investment to own during inflationary episodes. The three professors concluded, "When inflation has been moderate and stable, equities have performed relatively well. When there has been a leap in inflation, equities have performed less well in real terms. These sharp jumps in inflation are dangerous for investors."

> **In Summary**
> - Type-specific bonds and alternative asset classes perform better than the traditional asset classes (stocks, bonds, and cash) in inflationary environments.
> - Mild inflation can be positive for stocks; high inflation is not.

http://www.dailyfinance.com/2012/03/09/investing-error-stocks-not-inflation-hedge/

Rising Rate Bond Solutions

Inflation is one factor that can lead to rising rates. The Fed may attempt to slow down inflation, as Fed Chairman Volker did in the late 1970s. Therefore, we are going to transition from a discussion about inflation to rising rates. A recent Invesco analysis, which combines the two topics, provides a useful segue.

In their paper "When Yields Rise," Invesco looked at how different asset classes performed in various environments when rates rose. They state that interest rates tend to rise for three reasons: accelerating growth, accelerating inflation, or declining sovereign credit quality. The cause of rising rates is important because it affects the performance of various assets classes. For example, stocks tend to perform well when rates rise in response to accelerating growth, but they do not perform well when inflation accelerates or credit quality declines.

The Historical Behavior of Assets in Periods of Rising Rates

Rising Nominal Growth Primarily Due to:

	Real Growth	Inflation	Declining Creditworthiness
Gov't Bonds:	Down	Down	Down
Corp. Bonds:	N	N/Down	Down
Stocks:	Up	Down	Down
Commodities:	Up	Up	Up

Up = Asset tends to rise in value. Down = Asset tends to fall in value. N = Asset has had an ambiguous response to the scenario. Source: Invesco analysis. This table is intended to reflect the direction but not the magnitude of historic asset performance.

In summary, bonds tend not to perform well when rates rise for any of the three common reasons. Stocks perform well as long as rates rise due to real growth in the economy. However, commodities tend to be the best bet in all three scenarios.

Again, the conventional wisdom is to hold a portfolio of stocks and bonds. Rarely is there ever any mention of an asset class like commodities. However, if the next decade introduces us to elevated levels of inflation and/or rising rates, wouldn't the prudent course of action be to add these additional asset classes? I believe that the prudent course of action is to give these additional asset classes consideration. However, we cannot predict anything in the future with absolute certainty. Therefore, going "all in" on these new asset classes may not be sensible either. It may still make sense to maintain stock and bond exposure to some degree. For stock exposure, I might decide to introduce specific sectors of stocks and/or be more tactical with my exposure, increasing and decreasing as conditions warrant. I discuss both of these options in subsequent chapters. For bond exposure, we need to give extra consideration to the fact that a bear market for bonds may lie ahead. Instead of just holding a large general basket of bonds, we will want to be very specific to the type of bonds that warrant exposure in our portfolios. As a result, I have organized a type-specific pecking order below.

Best Bond Solutions: Although rising rates create massive headwinds for bonds in general, specific types of bonds will be less vulnerable in such an environment. Again, it is imperative to have a wide array of investment choices. Unfortunately, these choices are often not represented within the limited menu of options provided by most 401(k)s, 403(b)s, and 529 college savings plans.

The bottom line is that as rates rise, the prices on bonds will decrease. The change in price is a product of a technical term called "**duration**," which refers to the price sensitivity to a change in yield that varies across different types of bonds. As a general rule, a bond's duration is a factor of the bond's coupon (interest payment) and maturity (length of term). When the maturity is longer and the coupon is lower, the bond is more sensitive to changes in interest rates (i.e., higher duration).

As an example, a ten-year US Treasury note could have a duration of five, while the duration of a two-year high-yield corporate bond could have a duration of one. This means that for a one-basis-point increase in interest rates, the US Treasury note will lose five times as much value as the high-yield corporate bond. Therefore, rising rates will affect the price of all bonds, but the precise effects will differ depending on the bond's duration. For whatever percentage of your portfolio you believe should be allocated to bonds, we want to focus on bond asset classes that carry a lower risk of price decline in an environment of rising rates.

The list below exhibits the effect that an interest rate rise of 1 percent would have on various types of bonds.

1% Rise in interest rates:

1. Floating Rate = -0.1%
2. 2-Yr US Treasury = -2.0%
3. Convertibles = -3.0%
4. US Corporate High Yield = -4.2%
5. 5-Yr US Treasury = -4.7%
6. Emerging Market Debt = -5.4%
7. US Aggregate Index = -5.5%
8. Mortgage-Backed Securities = -6.1%

9.	TIPS	=	-6.4%
10.	Municipals	=	-7.5%
11.	10-Yr US Treasury	=	-8.5%
12.	30-Yr US Treasury	=	-16%

(Source: US Treasury, Barclays Capital, FactSet, J. P. Morgan Asset Management)

For example, an increase of 1 percent would decrease the price of a ten-year treasury bond by 8.5 percent. It would decrease a high-yield bond by 4.2 percent (6.7 year maturity), and it would decrease municipals by 7.5 percent (13.6-year maturity). The list is an extremely useful guide to follow when choosing various types of bonds for your portfolio when the threat of rising rates appears on the horizon. A take-away from this data for investors would be to **avoid bonds with higher duration during rising rate environments.** This is valuable information to know!

It is so valuable that the Financial Industry Regulatory Authority (FINRA) issued an alert about fixed income risks. In their article of caution to investors, titled "Duration – What an Interest Rate Hike Could Do to Your Bond Portfolio," a bond fund with ten-year duration "will decrease in value by 10 percent if interest rates rise 1 percent. On the other hand, the bond fund will increase in value by 10 percent if interest rates fall 1 percent. If a fund's duration is two years, then a rise of 1 percent in interest rates will result in a 2 percent decline in the bond fund's value. An increase of 2 percent in the bond's fund value would follow if interest rates fall by 1 percent."

Duration is the key concept here relating to bonds and interest rates. The good news is that you can look up your bond fund's average duration by viewing the fund's fact sheet on the fund company's website or by using other web-based research tools like Morningstar.

As you can see, a change of 1 percent in interest rates can have a significant impact on the value of bonds. The good news is that interest rates don't typically move a full percent at any point in time. Rather, they move in smaller increments. The bad news is that over a stretch of time, they can move much more than just 1 percent! You can now better understand why after thirty years of declining rates, and with there being nowhere else to go from here but up, we could see many years of higher rates ahead.

Welton Investment Corporation released a white paper titled "When Bonds Fall: How Risky Are Bonds if Interest Rates Rise?" In an attempt to anticipate what may be in our near future, they analyzed all historical data going back to 1919 and examined periods where interest rates rose more than 1.5 percent over a specific time span. In their words, "Whether slow and steady or sharp but short-lived, the answer is sobering—any meaningful rate increase from today's historically low levels would likely lead to significant losses."

Using past scenarios, they applied the slowest, fastest, and average rate increase scenarios at today's interest rate levels for a "single AAA corporate index of long duration." In their words, "Any rate increases from today's yield levels are likely to be accompanied by outsized losses. The slowest rate increase scenario is the most favorable of the three. It projects annual losses of just -.03 percent as coupon payments generally keep pace with capital losses. While investors avoid acute loss periods, this scenario also forecasts almost six years of near zero returns. The fastest rate increase scenario produces much sharper losses, while the average scenario (representing the average rise and length of each of the observed historical occurrences) produces annualized losses of -7.3 percent over about three years." Therefore, the best-case scenario is six long years of no return, and the average is three straight years of over 7 percent losses. Of course, past performance is no guarantee of future results. Therefore, it may be better, but it also could be worse!

Since rising rates are typically very bearish for bonds in general, the rankings to follow should not be viewed as endorsement. Rather, it is an exercise of highlighting type-specific bonds within the larger asset class. Assuming a rising rate environment, I have outlined the best options within what will be a less-than-optimal asset class.

Bond Option 1: Own Individual Bonds until Maturity

Rather than utilizing common mutual fund or ETF options to gain exposure to bonds, the other way to hold bonds in your portfolio is to actually purchase individual bonds. The benefit to this strategy is that if you hold the bond to maturity, which you have to be willing to do, you don't have to be as worried about declines in the price. What do I mean by this? If you purchase a ten-year bond from XYZ Company that promises to pay you a 4 percent coupon, you will receive 4 percent per year in income. After ten years, you will get your principal (a return on your original investment) back. If rates rise during the ten years you hold the bond, the value will drop. This will be unfortunate if you want to sell it. However, if you are willing to hold it until maturity and never sell it, the drop in price will be of no consequence to you.

Keep in mind that the original investment may have less purchasing power due to inflation over that time, but you are assured of not losing your principal due to rising rates. Of course, when purchasing individual bonds, it is important to heavily research the credit risk of the issuer. The chance that the issuer of the bond could default might be your greatest risk when buying individual issues.

Bond Option 2: Unconstrained Bonds

Instead of choosing a specific type of bond fund (i.e., a corporate bond fund or a government bond fund), a lot of value may be added by incorporating an unconstrained bond fund that can invest in any type of bond. Moreover, these bonds can actually short bonds (bet against them and profit on price declines) if need be. Therefore, you will not find this kind of strategy in an index fund. With a close to zero duration (that can even go negative through the use of shorting), this type of bond fund will not be nearly as interest-rate sensitive as most funds, if at all.

Considerations for gaining exposure to unconstrained bonds:

Mutual Fund: MainStay Unconstrained Bond MSYDX
Metropolitan West Unconstrained Bond MWCRX
Pimco Unconstrained Bond PUBDX

ETF: None

Bond Option 3: Floating-Rate Bonds

These bonds are well known for being better hedges than traditional corporate or government bonds in a rising rate environment. Unlike a traditional bond, which pays a fixed rate of interest, a floating-rate bond has a variable rate that resets regularly. The advantage of floating-rate bonds is that interest-rate risk is largely removed from the equation due to the constant resetting of rates, which these bonds can adapt to accordingly. While an owner of a fixed-rate bond can suffer if interest rates rise, floating-rate notes will pay higher yields if prevailing rates go up. Hence they tend to perform better than traditional bonds when interest rates are rising.

Considerations for gaining exposure to floating-rate bonds:

Mutual Funds: Eaton Vance Floating-Rate Adv (EABLX)
Fidelity Floating-Rate High Income (FFRHX)

ETFs: iShares Floating-Rate Note Fund (FLOT)
SPDR Barclays Capital Investment Grade Floating-Rate (FLRN)

Bond Option 4: Short-Term Bonds

Short-term bonds don't offer the same yields as their longer-term counterparts, but they provide more safety when rates start going up. Although they can be impacted by rising rates, the impact is much less than it is with longer-term bonds. Because they have a shorter term, the odds of a rate increase during their term are less. In addition, they are less interest-rate sensitive because the investor will get the face value of the bond back sooner, which can then be reinvested into bonds with the new higher rates.

Considerations for gaining exposure to short-term bonds:

Mutual Funds: Pimco Low Duration (PLDDX)
Vanguard Short-Term Bond Index (VBISX)

ETF: PIMCO Enhanced Short Maturity Strategy Fund ETF (MINT)
Vanguard Short-Term Bond ETF (BSV)

Bond Option 5: Convertible Bonds

Convertible bonds (convertibles) are types of bonds that the holder can convert into a specified number of shares of common stock in the issuing company or cash of equal value. The tradeoff to the investor for receiving the conversion feature results in typically lower interest payments tied to the bond. Companies like offering these bonds because of the lower required payments, and in the event that the investor converts to shares of stock, the company's debt disappears.

Considerations for gaining exposure to short-term bonds:

Mutual Funds: Vanguard Convertible Securities Inv (VCVSX)

ETF: SPDR Barclays Capital Convertible Secs (CWB)

Bond Option 6: High-Yield Bonds

High-yield bonds are on the riskier end of the fixed-income spectrum due to creditworthiness of the issuer. Therefore, it's somewhat counterintuitive that "riskier" bonds could outperform during periods of rising rates. However, the primary risk with high-yield bonds is credit risk. High-yield bonds, as a group, can actually hold up well when rates are rising because of their high yields (income they generate), which can be high enough to offset a decline in price.

Considerations for gaining exposure to high-yield bonds:

Mutual Funds: Fidelity High Income (SPHIX)
Vanguard High-Yield Corporate Inv (VWEHX)

ETFs: iShares iBoxx $ HY Corp Bond Fund ETF (HYG)
SPDR Barclays Capital High-Yield Bond ETF (JNK)

Bond Option 7: Emerging Market/Global Bonds

Like high-yield bonds, emerging market issues are more credit sensitive than they are rate sensitive. Here investors tend to look more at the underlying fiscal strength of the issuing country than they do the prevailing level of rates. As a result, improving global growth can be positive for debt in emerging markets, even though it typically leads to higher rates in the developed markets.

Considerations for gaining exposure to emerging market and global bonds:

Mutual Funds: Fidelity New Markets Income (FNMIX)
Templeton Global Bond (TPINX)

ETFs: iShares Emerging Markets High-Yield Bond ETF (EMHY)
Vanguard International Bond ETF (BNDX)

In summary
- In a rising rate environment, not all bonds will be affected the same (duration risk).
- If rates begin to rise, those who have access to type-specific bonds can better tailor their asset allocation over those who have limited bond offerings to choose from.

Fear rising with rates. Bond market sell-off likely a question of when, not if, and investors have no idea what's about to happen.

—Title of an *InvestmentNews* article by Andrew Osterland

CHAPTER 7

ALTERNATIVE INVESTING

Asset Allocation 2.0: Going beyond the typical sixty–forty portfolio. How colleges invest their endowment money

Question: Undoubtedly, some of the most intelligent people can be found in higher education. Therefore, if conventional wisdom of buying and holding a balanced portfolio is so wise, we must assume that colleges invest their endowments that way, right?

Some of the best returns over time have been produced not by popular mutual funds or hedge funds but by college endowments. Perhaps the most notable is that of Yale University. According to Mebane T. Faber's book *The Ivy Portfolio*, between 1985 and 2008 Yale had an average annual return of 16.62 percent, while the S&P 500 had returned 11.98 percent per year. Not only did Yale outperform the market over that time frame, but they also did it with 33 percent less volatility. Moreover, in the bear market years after the tech bubble burst, the S&P 500 declined by 30 percent from June 2000 to June 2003. At the same time, the Yale endowment gained roughly 20 percent, while Harvard's endowment was also positive with a 9 percent return.

> More specifics: From December 31, 2001, to December 31, 2010, an equal-weighted average of 460 university endowments returned 5 percent compared to the S&P 500 Index average return of -1.6 percent. Source: 2010 NACUBO Endowment Study, Annual Report of the National Association of College and University Business Officers of Endowment Performance and Management in Higher Education, 2011.

What is their secret sauce? How are these endowments able to outperform and do so with less risk? The answer is **alternative investments**.

Definition of alternative investment: Alternative asset classes, or alts for short, are investments in asset classes that go beyond the typical stocks, bonds, and cash. In this arena you will find terms like futures, commodities, hedge funds, private equity, long/short, and absolute return.

Alternatives typically fall under one of three different umbrellas:

1. Nontraditional asset classes (such as commodities and currencies)
2. Nontraditional strategies (such as shorting or hedging)
3. Illiquid assets (such as private equity and private debt)

How important is the utilization of alternatives for some of the best-run portfolios? One only needs to look at college endowment funds to see how some of the biggest and best-run portfolios manage their money. A quick Google search yields some immediate results and annual reports.

In full disclosure, I did not choose these schools because they support the thesis of this chapter. Rather, they were some of the most recognizable names that came up on the first page of my Google search.

Take, for example, the weighted average allocations for all of the **University of California** schools (Berkeley, Davis, Irvine, Los Angeles, Merced, Riverside, San Diego, San Francisco, Santa Barbara, and Santa Cruz) as of June 30, 2011:

- **Stocks:** 38 percent (includes US Equity, Non-US Equity, and Global Equity)
- **Bonds:** 13.6 percent (includes US Fixed Income and Non-US Fixed Income)
- **Alternatives:** 45 percent (includes Absolute Return, Real Estate, Private Equity, and Commodities)
- **Cash: 3.3 percent**

Dartmouth College's allocations, as of June 30, 2011:

- **Stocks: 30.2 percent** (includes US Equity, International Equity, and Emerging Market Equity)
- **Bonds: 2 percent** (includes US Fixed-Income and US TIPS—Treasury Inflation Protected Securities)
- **Alternatives: 63 percent** (includes Marketable Alternative Equity, Private Equity, Venture Capital, Real Estate, and Commodities)
- **Cash: 4.8 percent**

Yale University's allocations, as of June 30, 2011:

- **Stocks: 15.7 percent** (includes Domestic Equity and Foreign Equity)
- **Bonds: 3.9 percent** (labeled as Fixed Income)
- **Alternatives: 81.5 percent** (includes Absolute Return, Private Equity, and Real Assets)
- **Cash: -1.1** (as listed in the report)

Notice how little the endowments have allocated to common stocks and bonds? How does that compare to the asset allocation model we ran using *Money* magazine's allocator in chapter three? That is a big difference from the conventional wisdom that individual investors have been taught. The big boys are doing one thing, while the little guys (you and me) are encouraged to do another.

To be fair, it isn't entirely the little guy's fault for not having exposure to these other asset classes. Most of these investments were not available for purchase in liquid, low-minimum, prepackaged options for the individual investor. However, things are beginning to change, as many of these strategies are now more accessible through mutual funds and ETFs.

Lipper conducted a study that analyzed how adding alternatives to a portfolio changes that portfolio's specific risk/return characteristics for the decade December 31, 2000–December 31, 2010. Using standard deviation as a measure of risk (and volatility), they found the following:

Portfolio 1	**Portfolio 2**	**Portfolio 3**
60 percent Stocks	40 percent Stocks	30 percent Stocks
35 percent Bonds	35 percent Bonds	35 percent Bonds
5 percent Cash	5 percent Cash	5 percent Cash
0 percent Alternatives	20 percent Alternatives	30 percent Alternatives
Return: **4.85 percent**	Return: **5.41 percent**	Return: **5.78 percent**
Risk: **11.03 percent**	Risk: **7.73 percent**	Risk: **6.49 percent**

*Risk = Standard Deviation

(Source: Investopedia)

As you can see by the chart above, portfolio 1 on the left, which looks more similar to our *Money* magazine asset allocation comprising mostly stocks and bonds, exhibited a ten-year average annual return of 4.85 with a standard deviation (a measurement of risk) of 11.03 percent. If a 20 percent

Alternative Investing

alternatives allocation is added to the portfolio, exemplified in the middle chart, we see the annual return increase to 5.41 percent and the risk level reduced a good amount by almost 30 percent (11.03 versus 7.73) with standard deviation at 7.73 percent. If we add 30 percent alternatives, the numbers continue to improve, as seen in the column to the right. Average annual return increases and risk decreases even further.

> You can view an informational ten-minute video, in which Ben Stein explains alternatives, here: https://www.myeliteaccess.com/eliteaccess/Index.jsp

Core Alternatives

Instead of providing an entire book on alternatives, I am going to focus on the five categories that I feel might add the most value to the individual investor moving forward, including selection, availability, liquidity, etc. What these solutions offer the investor is not only the ability to achieve growth (play offense) but also the ability to help reduce the drawdowns of stock market declines (play defense) when these are added to the investor's portfolio.

1. Long/Short
2. Market Neutral
3. Commodities
4. Precious Metals
5. Managed Futures

Long/Short (Defense via Shorting)

Managers of long/short strategies can go long (bet on an uptrend) and hedge against the market declines through options or shorting securities (bet on a downtrend), hence the title long/short. The simplified explanation is that a money manager can bet against an investment, such as a stock or an index, and profit when it declines. The concept of shorting is not one that many average investors are aware of. However, I have found that many people's eyes widen and their ears perk up when introduced to this concept. 2008 is still fresh in many people's memory and the helpless feelings they experienced as they were instructed to ride it out. Strategies that can help defend against the downward blows of another bear market are often well received.

> For a more detailed overview of the shorting process, consider watching this short informational video: http://www.investopedia.com/video/play/short-selling/.

Although short selling isn't always profitable, it does arm us with another tool in our toolbox. It helps us combat both bear market declines and overall portfolio volatility.

Imagine money managers sifting through company profiles and accounting reports. They obviously like the stocks that exist within their portfolio, but there must be an equal number of companies that they dislike and perhaps would want to bet against. Funds that allow shorting give managers the green light to take advantage of such an opportunity.

What you will most commonly notice with many long/short funds is that they don't entirely eliminate the potential for negative returns in a severe bear market, but they can dramatically reduce the amount of loss. Conversely, in great bull runs, they may not capture all of the upside, but they can capture a good portion of the gains. In summary, they can reduce the total volatility of the portfolio, thereby creating a smoother sailing experience for the investor that is similar to stabilizers on a cruise ship.

Alternative Investing

Consider the following returns for some of the more popular long/short funds in the bear and bull markets of 2008 and 2009 (represented by Vanguard's S&P 500 Index fund):

	2008	2009
Vanguard 500 Index Inv (VFINX):	-37.02 percent	26.49 percent
Diamond Hill Long-Short A (DIAMX):	-23.65 percent	17.93 percent
Gateway (GATEX):	-13.92 percent	6.57 percent
Marketfield (MFNDX):	-13.10 percent	30.76 percent
Pimco EqS Long/Short (PMHDX):	-4.88 percent	20.87 percent
Wasatch Long/Short Investor (FMLSX):	-20.93 percent	30.07 percent

Note: All these funds dramatically reduced the stock market drawdown in 2008, and some continued to then outperform to the upside in 2009. We have emphasized these two years to keep the analysis less cumbersome and to put extra highlighting on major bear markets, which trigger the most emotions and the generally worst investment decisions for the small investor.

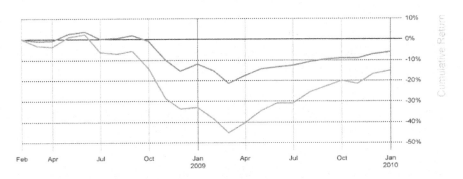

This graph shows how even the Gateway fund (top line), which is the *worst* performer of the group, outperformed the S&P 500 (bottom line) over those two years, even with only a modest gain in 2009. How was this possible? They managed downside risk. One calendar year with a major drawdown can really set a portfolio back.

For more exposure to the long/short strategy, I recommend Mainstay Marketfield (MFNDX) or Pimco EqS Long/Short (PMHDX).

Market Neutral (Defense via Shorting)

Market neutral is a strategy related to long/short. It utilizes the same techniques (going long or short investments), but it is managed with a different mandate, and thus it behaves in its own unique way. In general, this strategy often involves taking matching long and short positions in different yet similar stocks to increase the return from making good stock selections and to decrease the return from broad market movements. For example, with this strategy, fund managers find pairs of stocks with a high correlation to each other, and then they go long (bet stock goes up) with the one they deem most attractive and short (bet stock goes down) with the one they deem least attractive.

Take Coke and Pepsi as examples. Both of these stocks are in the same industry and will therefore be highly correlated to each other (move in unison). However, they are two different companies and their correlation will not be exactly 1:1; they will exhibit slight differences (unique movements). In this example the managers may go long Coca Cola and short Pepsi. If both Coke and Pepsi go up in a bull market, they will make money on Coke and lose money on Pepsi. Their hope is that Coke will appreciate a bit more than they will lose on their Pepsi short (called the spread, or the difference between their upside bet against their downside hedge). If they both go down, theoretically they will lose money on Coke and make money on Pepsi. They will hope to earn more on the decline of Pepsi than on their loss on Coke. The goal is to generate consistently moderate returns in both up and down markets.

Alternative Investing

Unlike the previous long/short strategy, which has a relatively high correlation (for alternatives) to the overall market, the market-neutral strategy utilizes going long and short to various positions in a manner that exhibits little correlation to the overall market. As a result, the performance is fairly consistent. It never achieves large gains, but it also avoids large losses. This type of long/short strategy may be best suited for conservative investors who do not wish to experience higher volatility levels produced from the other four alternative options.

For exposure to market-neutral strategies, I recommend the Arbitrage Fund (ARBFX) and the Merger Fund (MERFX), both of which have produced very consistent annual returns.

Consider the following returns for market-neutral funds in the bear and bull markets of 2008 and 2009:

	2008	2009
Vanguard 500 Index Inv (VFINX):	**-37.02 percent**	**26.49 percent**
Arbitrage (ARBFX):	-0.63 percent	10.05 percent
Merger (MERFX):	-2.86 percent	8.52 percent

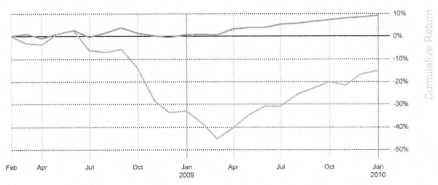

Like the previous scenario involving the long/short Gateway fund, you can witness similar results by comparing the market-neutral Merger fund, which had the *least impressive* results of the two options, to the Vanguard 500 Index fund from 2008 to 2009. It shows how the Merger fund (top line) outperformed the S&P 500 (bottom line) over those two years, even with only a modest gain in 2009. Again, how is this possible? They managed downside risk.

Commodities (Defense via Low Correlation to other Asset Classes)

Commodity funds provide exposure to price movements in numerous commodities, typically through the use of derivatives. While these funds can have high volatility, they also tend to have a low correlation to stocks and bonds, and they tend to hedge a portfolio's inflation risk. In other words, as a stand-alone investment option it is very volatile, but as a portion of the portfolio it will reduce the volatility of the portfolio as a whole.

Analogy: Eat a jalapeno by itself and you will get a volatile experience in your mouth. However, if you mix the jalapeno with a pot of chili, it will add flavor and value to your eating experience. The key is the right combination of ingredients.

Some examples of commodities are as follows:

- Cattle
- Cocoa
- Coffee
- Copper
- Corn
- Cotton
- Gold
- Lead
- Lean Hogs
- Lumber

- Natural Gas
- Nickel
- Oats
- Oil
- Orange Juice
- Palladium
- Platinum
- Pork Bellies
- Rough Rice
- Silver
- Soybeans
- Sugar
- Wheat
- Zinc

This asset class is known as a good inflation hedge, since with inflation (higher prices) the cost of your everyday purchases (gas, corn, coffee, etc.) goes up in addition to your investment. Moreover, due to its low correlation with stocks and bonds, this asset class is a good diversifier from the traditional asset classes.

For exposure to a broad basket of commodities, I recommend Pimco Commodity Real Return Strategy (PCRDX) mutual fund and/or the PowerShares DB Commodity Index Tracking Fund (DBC) ETF. One note of caution is that DBC may require the investor to file a K-1 tax form with the IRS (consult with your tax advisor), and it may be best held within a tax-deferred account, such as an IRA.

Precious Metals (Defense via Low Correlation)

Another very specific type of investment that you should consider for the overall portfolio is a subset of the alternative asset class: commodities. Many people also view these precious metals as a currency. I believe it is prudent to hold precious metals in addition to general commodities for three reasons:

1. If we truly are seeking a smoother ride with our investment portfolios, we need to have low correlation assets. Precious metals provide us access to an asset class that historically has little correlation to the other major stock and bond asset classes.
2. If in the future inflation begins to increase, historically speaking, metals tend to perform well.
3. You should hold precious metals as insurance against the devaluing of paper (fiat) currencies around the world. Easy monetary policies are prevalent not just at home but on a global scale.

A couple of pertinent quotes on the matter:

On September 4, 2012, "Bond King" Bill Gross tweeted, "Draghi appears willing to write two- to three-year 'checks' to peripherals. Very reflationary. Buy gold, TIPS, real assets." *Note: the European Central Bank (ECB) president is Mario Draghi.

This tweet made its rounds in the financial blogs, which led to *Bloomberg* interviewing Gross. In this interview, Gross elaborated on his recommendation to purchase real assets, especially gold:

"Gold can't be reproduced. It could certainly be taken out of the ground in an increasing rate, but there's a limited amount of gold. And there has been an unlimited amount of paper money over the past twenty to thirty years, and now—in this period of central bank expansion, where it's QE1 or QE2, or whether it's the LTROs with the ECB or this potential new program. Central banks are at their leisure to basically print money. Gold is a fixed commodity that has a considerable store of value that paper money has not. When a central bank starts writing checks and printing money in the trillions of dollars, it's best to have something that's tangible and can't be reproduced, such as gold."

The recommendation that Gross makes is noteworthy because he is advising investors to reallocate to asset classes that aren't available within his company's managed funds. Pimco doesn't have a gold alternative for investors to utilize. He does mention their commodity fund, but that isn't a pure gold play, and he even mentions utilizing a gold ETF. Therefore, he is advising investors to utilize something that his company does not offer. This is a very rare occurrence on financial television. This honesty emphasizes the truth of his opinion, which is certainly unbiased.

http://www.washingtonsblog.com/2012/09/the-bond-king-buy-gold-not-bonds.html

As a result of all of this, many central banks and countries like China and Russia are greatly increasing their purchases of precious metals, which have the highest amounts since 1964. Why is this the case? To quote from the article in the *New American*, "The central bank buying spree was led by monetary authorities in Russia, Brazil, Iraq, and other developing nations. Analysts said the exploding demand was part of a worldwide effort to diversify away from the troubled US dollar and the severely embattled euro as the global economy continues to struggle, with more than a few experts harping on so-called 'currency wars' as central bankers race to devalue their fiat currencies through inflation of the currency supply."

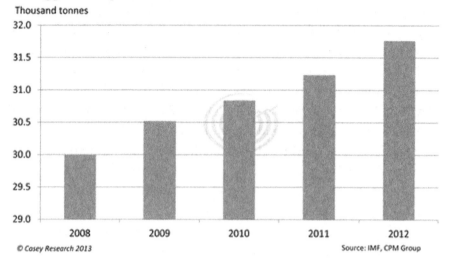

(Source: Casey Research)

http://www.thenewamerican.com/economy/markets/item/14595-amid-record-demand-in-2012-central-banks-scramble-to-buy-gold

Many investors don't know how to invest, or the most efficient way to invest in precious metals. *I wouldn't recommend* purchasing a precious metals mutual fund. Many fund families offer a fund that has a title that would lead you to believe it provides precious metal exposure, but almost all of them are mostly comprised of metal-mining company stocks. In other words, the majority of "precious metal" mutual funds' price movements are not directly tied to the price of the metal. The one exception is the Gold Bullion Strategy Investor fund (QGLDX) that was birthed in 2013. I would recommend considering one of the following:

Alternative Investing

1. You could purchase physical gold and silver (coins, bars, etc.) and store them in a safe and secure location. This may be appropriate for a very small portion of your exposure.
2. You could get ETFs (exchange traded funds). The most popular ETFs that allow investors exposure to the price of metals are SPDR Gold Trust (GLD), iShares Gold Trust (IAU), and iShares Silver Trust (SLV).
3. Closed-end funds are similar to open-ended mutual funds in that they offer shares and trades on an exchange. The major difference is that they only offer a set number of shares, unlike open-ended funds, which increase or decrease the number that is available, depending on when investors purchase and sell the fund. Popular closed-end options include Central Fund of Canada (CEF), Central GoldTrust (GTU), Sprott Physical Gold Trust (PHYS), and Sprott Physical Silver Trust (PSLV).

I personally own and recommend CEF and GTU. Some may think that I am splitting hairs by choosing the closed-end fund option over the ETF, but I did so for three reasons:

1. Some investors who hold the closed-end fund options within a taxable account for one year and then sell, realizing long-term capital gains, are currently taxed at the maximum rate of 20 percent instead of the 28 percent applied against most precious metals ETFs and physical coins, which are taxed as collectibles. This qualification for the lower tax rate is because of a special election called a qualified electing fund for passive foreign investment companies.
2. For what it is worth, I would prefer to have the metals held in a vault in Canada, as opposed to across the ocean

in London. The closed-end fund options that I have mentioned include the Central Fund of Canada (CEF), Central GoldTrust (GTU), Sprott Physical Gold Trust (PHYS), Sprott Physical Silver Trust (PSLV), and Sprott Physical Platinum & Palladium Trust (SPPP). These offerings are regularly audited and held in a secure storage location in Canada.
3. Since 1961, the Central Fund of Canada (CEF) has had a consistent track record of stability and trustworthiness.

Managed Futures (Defense via Shorting and Low Correlation)

Managed futures typically represent contracts to buy or sell commodities, currencies, or interest rates at a future date. In terms of portfolio construction, one of their best attributes is the fact that they are usually not correlated with traditional asset classes like stocks and bonds. They can profit in both rising and falling markets because they can be long and/or short, as evidenced in the following annual returns. Lastly, they can prove beneficial in both inflationary and deflationary environments because they can be long or short asset classes like commodities (inflation hedge) or US treasuries (deflation hedge). They also tend to follow an unemotional systematic trend-following system, which we will discuss in more detail in chapter nine. In terms of all our discussions about alternatives up until now, managed futures play the role of a Swiss Army knife, combining long/short strategies with commodities. Its diverse alternative philosophy makes it the perfect alternative investment.

The Altegris 40 Index tracks the performance of the forty leading managed futures programs, as tracked by Altegris Clearing Solutions each month. The index has been active since January 1990. Below are the annual returns as reported by Altegris and compared to the Vanguard 500 Index.

	Altegris 40 Index	versus	Vanguard 500 Index Inv.
1998:	12.61 percent		28.62 percent
1999:	.87 percent		21.07 percent
2000:	10.63 percent		-9.06 percent
2001:	5.39 percent		-12.02 percent
2002:	15.22 percent		-22.15 percent
2003:	15.99 percent		28.50 percent
2004:	2.57 percent		10.74 percent
2005:	4.51 percent		4.77 percent
2006:	6.70 percent		15.64 percent
2007:	7.18 percent		5.39 percent
2008:	15.47 percent		-37.02 percent
2009:	-7.98 percent		26.49 percent
2010:	11.33 percent		14.91 percent
2011:	-3.23 percent		1.97 percent
2012:	-4.75 percent		15.82 percent
2013:	-2.45 percent		32.18 percent

A couple of takeaways from these numbers:

1. Managed futures are uncorrelated with stocks. They exhibited positive returns in the bear markets between 2000 and 2002 and in 2008, when stocks suffered steep declines. Conversely, in the most recent bull run in stocks, managed futures have underperformed.
2. The downside drawdown hasn't been nearly as great as that of stocks (i.e., no years with double-digit declines).

For exposure to managed futures, I recommend AQR Managed Futures Strategy Inv (AQMNX) and/or WisdomTree Managed Futures (WDTI) for an ETF option.

Alternative-Like Options

Below, I have listed other alternative-like options for additional consideration. Each possesses its own unique features and benefits.

1. **Master Limited Partnerships (MLPs)**
2. **Real Estate Investment Trusts (REITs)**
3. **ETFs and Low-Volatility ETFs**
4. **Structured Notes**

These aren't typically classified as alternative investments. However, these four types of investments are unique and specific in their own right, and they deserve consideration. Because they diverge a bit from the norm than the more conventional choices, I have decided to include them in this chapter.

The first two, MLPs and REITs, are types of stocks that are unique because of their ability to generate income. This can be useful if income-producing bonds go out of favor. The second two are more volatility (risk) insulators. If this low interest rate environment continues for some time, then investors may be forced into more aggressive options. For those that are more averse to risk, these two types of investments may help buffer the volatility of more aggressive options. All four of these options (with possibly the exception of REITs) are typically not found in most conventional portfolios such as 401(k)s, 403(b)s, and 529 plans.

Master Limited Partnerships (MLPs) (Defense via Lower Correlation and Income Producing)

Master limited partnerships (MLPs) are publicly traded companies in the "midstream energy transportation" industry. In other words, they transport oil and natural gas (natural resource pipeline outlets). It is a relatively new asset class that was birthed from the 1986 Tax Reform Act.

It should be noted that although MLPs operate within a subset of the energy industry, they are somewhat agnostic toward price. In other words, they simply generate revenue by transporting the resource. The price of oil and/or natural gas might be high or low, but this makes very little difference to the MLP.

Regarding the previous themes of inflation and rising rates, these investments provide an inflation hedge, as the rent on their pipes is usually indexed to the producer price index (PPI) to guarantee an inflation-protected stream of income. However, the performance in a rising-rate environment is less predictable and may depend on the speed of the rises. If the rates are increased at a slow and steady pace, it may have only minimal impact. On the other hand, if rates rise too fast, they will most likely create a temporary decline in the price of the MLP. Of course, at the same time, many assets will decline if rates rise too quickly. Therefore, MLPs, along with traditional stocks and bonds, will hope that the Fed can gradually lead us into a rising rate environment.

> **Taxing Matters**
>
> 1. MLPs do not have to pay corporate taxes, and they are required to distribute most of their profits to owners of MLP shares (partners), which contributes to the high yields. Distributions are considered a return of capital, which means that there are no taxes on most returns until the investor sells the MLP. These features are alluring for those seeking income from their taxable accounts.
>
> 2. One caveat: certain shares of MLPs will generate a K-1 tax form, which can add to accounting fees and delay filing. In addition, if an MLP operates in numerous states, you may be required to file a return with each, and this can lead to additional costs. Consult with your tax advisor when considering this type of investment.

> 3. Depending on the financial instrument that the investor chooses, MLPs can provide some very unique tax implications. If held in a tax-deferred account, such as an IRA, there most likely won't be any tax implications. However, if the investment produces a K-1, such as the ETF Alerian MLP Index, then the portion of the distributions designated as "ordinary income" may be considered unrelated business taxable income (UBTI) and subject to taxation. UBTI is usually a small percentage of total distributions, and it will not be taxed as long as the amount of this income and all other sources of UBTI do not exceed one thousand dollars in any year.

We are dealing with a relatively new asset class that has strong growth potential for the future, has a durable business model, generates high yields in a low-yield environment, can provide tax advantages within a taxable account, has built-in inflation protection, and carries a relatively low correlation to the general stock market compared to other equity asset classes. Because of this, MLPs may be an attractive asset class moving forward.

> A five-minute video explaining MLPs can be found here: http://www.youtube.com/watch?v=SgpJ8SoSDpk.

For MLP investment exposure, I recommend Oppenheimer SteelPath MLP Select 40 Fund MLPFX (1099 filing) or the Alerian MLP Index ETF AMLP (potential K-1 filing).

Real Estate Investment Trusts (REITs) (Defense via Lower Correlation and Income Producing)

A real estate investment trust (REIT) is a company that owns and manages income-producing real estate. In 1960, an act of Congress created REITs to enable large and small investors alike to enjoy rental income from commercial property. REITs are governed by many regulations. Most importantly, they must distribute at least 90 percent of their taxable income to shareholders each year as a dividend. Essentially they collect rent (a good inflation hedge) and pay that out to shareholders.

REITs can invest in a variety of property types. Nearly two-thirds of the investments are in offices, apartments, shopping centers, regional malls, and industrial facilities. The rest is divided among hotels, self-storage facilities, health care properties, and some specialty REITs that own things like prisons, theaters, golf courses, and timberlands.

Why REITs warrant some consideration for your portfolio can best be explained by a report produced by NAREIT (National Association of Real Estate Investment Trusts). NAREIT published data that analyzed how a 10-percent REIT exposure to a classic sixty–forty portfolio would have increased the overall return without adding any risk. From December 1991 through December 2011, the portfolio with the REIT exposure returned 8.1 percent versus 7.6 percent, while both portfolios carried a risk level of 9.6 percent. REITs have been able to help control risk to a certain degree because of their high dividend yield and lower levels of correlation with other asset classes, as we outline in the second subsequent chart (note: REIT, MLP, and gold low correlations to conventional asset classes).

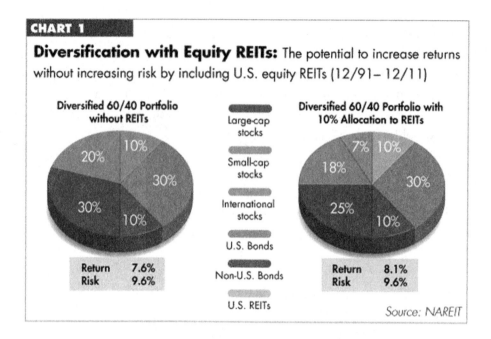

http://www.advisorone.com/2012/08/23/four-reasons-reits-belong-in-retirement-portfolios?t=alternative-investments.

Long Term: November 2003 to April 2012	Alerian MLP	FTSE NAREIT All REITs	DJ Select Micro Cap	S&P Pref Stock	BarCap US Treas TIPS	BarCap US Corp Hi Yld	S&P GSCI Gold	IA SBBI S&P 500	IA SBBI US LT Govt
Alerian MLP	1	—	—	—	—	—	—	—	—
FTSE NAREIT All REITs	0.39	1	—	—	—	—	—	—	—
DJ Select Micro Cap	0.42	0.81	1	—	—	—	—	—	—
S&P Preferred Stock	0.54	0.52	0.5	1	—	—	—	—	—
BarCap US Treasury US TIPS	0.12	0.28	0.1	0.25	1	—	—	—	—
BarCap US Corporate High Yield	0.63	0.73	0.68	0.57	0.39	1	—	—	—
S&P GSCI Gold	0.03	0.15	0.07	0	0.47	0.14	1	—	—
IA SBBI S&P 500	0.49	0.8	0.9	0.58	0.21	0.74	0.11	1	—
IA SBBI US LT Govt	−0.44	−0.07	−0.25	−0.03	0.52	−0.23	0.2	−0.22	1

http://www.aaii.com/journal/article/the-alternative-portfolio-diversifying-away-from-a-traditional-allocation.mobile

Considerations for gaining exposure to REITs:

Mutual Funds: T. Rowe Price Real Estate (TRREX)
Vanguard REIT Index Inv (VGSIX)

ETFs: SPDR Dow Jones REIT (RWR)
Vanguard REIT Sector (VNQ)

In sum, MLPs and REITs provide higher than average income for stock positions. They are niche stock sectors, and they provide further diversification within your portfolios. Both will provide lower than average correlation to the overall market compared to other stocks (MLPs slightly more than REITs). Lastly, they each have some inherent inflation protection due to the rental income features within their design.

Low-Volatility ETFs (Defense via Volatility Reduction)

As we examined earlier, volatility (large price swings/fluctuations) don't mix well with the emotions of investors. This tends to lead to poor decisions. One relatively new solution that may help alleviate this conundrum is the low-volatility ETF.

As an example, a low-volatility ETF may buy the one hundred least volatile stocks in the index based on standard deviation measure over the past twelve months. The stocks with the lowest volatility get the highest weightings within the portfolio. The holdings are reoptimized quarterly, and the ETF removes the stocks whose volatilities have increased in favor of those that have decreased.

The always important relationship we consistently reference is the risk to return ratio. As it pertains to low-volatility ETFs, we know there are intrinsic risk measures within the strategy design. However, what about performance in conjunction with risk management? Is it possible to keep pace with the market with less risk by just purchasing the least volatile stocks? If you consider a long enough period of time, that is what history suggests. According to a *Wall Street Journal* article from October 1, 2011, "The low-volatility index has returned 80 percent during the past ten years, compared with the S&P 500's 42.9 percent, assuming reinvested dividends. Go back twenty years, a period that includes most of the go-go 1990s, and the index has beaten the S&P 500 by about 180 percentage points, according to S&P, which set up the low-volatility index in April."

The article continues to say, "Academic research suggests that the low-volatility strategy has worked for even longer periods. The least-volatile quintile of the one thousand biggest stocks in the United States returned 10.2 percent annually from 1968 to 2010, while the most volatile quintile gained 6.6 percent, according to Brendan Bradley of Acadian Asset Management in Boston, who earlier this year published a study on the returns of low-volatility stocks with Malcolm Baker of Harvard University and Jeffrey Wurgler of New York University in the *Financial Analysts Journal*. The US stock market overall returned 9.6 percent during the same period."

Of course, nothing will always outperform. In fact, in 2009, the S&P 500 gained 26.5 percent, while the low-volatility index gained only 19.2 percent (although not bad). In addition, in the eight years leading up to the dot-com peak in March 2000, the low-volatility index gained less than half of the S&P 500. In major bull markets, when high-volatility stocks tend to outpace, this type of strategy may underperform. As we discussed earlier, money managers typically determine whether it was a good year or a bad year in relation to the benchmark that they are tracking. I think many investors with a more conservative risk tolerance would be happy with a return of over 19 percent.

A consistent theme throughout this book is to seek strong returns in bull markets but to employ risk management strategies to help buffer downside risk. Therefore, I consider low-volatility ETFs to be useful investment innovations that are tailor made to the average American's emotional risk tolerance to stocks.

http://online.wsj.com/article/SB10001424052970203405504576599031270062 12.html

Low-volatility ETF options from PowerShares:

SPLV: PowerShares S&P 500 Low-Volatility Portfolio
XSLV: PowerShares S&P Small-Cap Low-Volatility Portfolio
XMLV: S&P Mid-Cap Low-Volatility Portfolio
EELV: S&P Emerging Markets Low-Volatility Portfolio
IDLV: S&P International Developed Low-Volatility Portfolio

Low-volatility ETF options from iShares:

USMV: iShares MSCI USA Minimum-Volatility ETF
ACWV: iShares MSCI All Country World Minimum-Volatility ETF
EFAV: iShares MSCI EAFE Minimum-Volatility ETF
EEMV: iShares MSCI Emerging Markets Minimum-Volatility ETF
For investors who are more adverse to volatility but desire stock exposure in their portfolios, low-volatility ETFs may be a good consideration.

*More low-volatility ETFs exist and new ones are coming to the market regularly.

Structured Notes (Defense via Options/Downside Reduction)

For investors who appreciate the attributes of low-volatility ETFs, another consideration for their portfolios could be structured notes. These investments are similar to CDs (certificates of deposit) in that large banks issue them for specific lengths of time, such as eighteen months, three years, or five years. However, the similarities end there.

> *Investopedia* describes a structured note as: "A hybrid security that attempts to change its profile by including additional modifying structures. A simple example would be a five-year bond tied together with an option contract. This structure would work to increase the bond's returns."

Essentially, the banks are able to package multiple investments together to provide an investor with a sophisticated solution to regulate investment risk. Although they come in many varieties, I will highlight two of the more basic and widely implemented strategies.

Perhaps these are best explained by walking through a couple of examples on how they work.

Hypothetical Example 1: Bank ABC offers a three-year "buffered uncapped market participation security linked to the S&P 500 Index."

Offered in $1,000 increments, this three-year note offers the upside appreciation on the S&P 500, from the starting point to the ending point, which is called point to point. In addition, it provides a *20 percent buffer to the downside.*

Hypothetical example:

S&P 500 Index Return	Investor Participation	Investor's Return
20 percent	100 percent Upside	20 percent
5 percent	100 percent Upside	5 percent
-5 percent	Buffer of 20 percent	0 percent
-20 percent	Buffer of 20 percent	0 percent
-30 percent	1X loss beyond buffer	-10 percent
-45 percent	1X loss beyond buffer	-25 percent

As you can see, if the S&P 500 had a positive return over that three-year time frame, then the structured note will deliver the same return to the investor. However, if there is a decline by the index at the end of the three-year time period, the investor will be buffered by 20 percent on any potential loss.

The structured note may be a better investment for investors who know that they will not be selling their S&P 500 investment in the next three years but would like the added comfort of knowing that there is a buffer to help protect them against some downside risk.

The following questions might be raised: "Why wouldn't everyone want to use structured notes? Why would anyone just buy and hold the index, which has no downside protection?" The answer is that the investor has to assume issuer risk. If Bank ABC (from our example) goes bankrupt during the term of the note, then the investor may lose his or her principal. The odds may be slim of this occurring, but it cannot be dismissed. In addition, the investor only capitalizes on price appreciation, not dividend income. Lastly, this is not a very liquid investment. If you wish to sell your note before the term ends, you will have to do so in a secondary market and therefore may have to take a discount to liquidate.

For those who like the concept of structured notes but require additional guarantees, some issues do qualify for FDIC protection. Since they can provide the investor the best safety reassurance possible that they will not lose their money, they are naturally managed very conservatively. But they can offer upside opportunity that is greater than a certificate of deposit, while still providing downside protection. You might find a feature like that on a product that is similar to the next hypothetical example.

Hypothetical Example 2: Bank XYZ offers a five-year ETF asset allocation CD

It is a five-year investment sold in $1,000 increments. It offers upside potential of a diversified portfolio with the guarantee of principal protection. The bank dynamically allocates among approximately a dozen different ETFs and is adjusted monthly with a goal of limiting portfolio volatility (not for aggressive growth).

The hypothetical example below is based on a $1,000 investment:

ETF Portfolio Return	Investor Participation	Investor's Return
80 percent	100 percent Upside	80 percent
50 percent	100 percent Upside	50 percent
30 percent	100 percent Upside	30 percent
10 percent	100 percent Upside	10 percent
0 percent	100 percent Upside	0 percent
-10 percent	0 percent Downside	0 percent
-20 percent	0 percent Downside	0 percent
-30 percent	0 percent Downside	0 percent
-80 percent	0 percent Downside	0 percent

Here you can see that if the note is held to maturity, the investor has no downside risk. The investor only has upside potential!

In sum, these vehicles allow investors to purchase conservative (FDIC insured) to aggressive strategies that provide some added peace of mind with their downside protection features. Like CDs, they are designed for investors to hold them for specific lengths of time and don't need short-term liquidity. Therefore, these products almost force investors to buy and hold them to reap the benefits. This may be beneficial to admittedly undisciplined investors.

As you can see, there are many different asset classes and investment approaches that are unique and may be able to add value to your portfolio. You might have never heard of some of the strategies mentioned in this chapter as they get little mainstream press, but that is the point. With conventional strategies at risk of struggling into the future, we need to keep an open mind and explore all options.

A Better Balanced Portfolio

The 7Twelve Portfolio

Up to this point you have been introduced to numerous asset classes and strategies beyond the simple sixty–forty portfolio. I have argued that we need additional solutions more sophisticated than this classic strategy. However, perhaps the simplicity of the two asset class portfolio appeals to you. The idea that you only need to own a couple of investments and never need to make adjustments except for the occasional rebalancing may be the type of strategy you want. However, we have to ask, can we do better than this? Is there an easy way to combine some of the ideas in this book in a simple, balanced fashion that could possibly improve our long-term performance? I think the answer is yes, and I think it has been best answered by Professor Craig L. Israelsen, who developed what is called the 7Twelve Portfolio.

The name 7Twelve is derived from its components, which are twelve selected funds within seven core asset classes, as represented on the following chart.

Alternative Investing

7Twelve® Balanced Portfolio

Approximately 65% of the Allocation in Equity and Diversifying Assets				Approximately 35% of the Allocation in Bonds and Cash			
US Equity	Non-US Equity	Real Estate	Resources	US Bonds	Non-US Bonds	Cash	
Large Companies	Developed Markets	Real Estate	Natural Resources	US Aggregate Bonds	International Bonds	US Money Market
Medium-sized Companies	Emerging Markets		Commodities	Inflation Protected Bonds (TIPS)		
Small Companies						

A major theme of this book is to consider alternative asset classes and strategies beyond just US stocks and US bonds. Some of the categories will be familiar to you by now (i.e., real estate, natural resources, commodities, inflation protected securities, and international bonds). Israelsen combines all of these along with emerging markets and the more traditional asset classes in equal weights. This unique combination births a unique portfolio that is similar to our classic balanced portfolio in that it is 65 percent equities, 35 percent bonds, and 5 percent cash, but when examined further, the specific underlying ingredients are more numerous and specific.

A comparison of how the classic model looks compared to the new 7Twelve balanced portfolio:

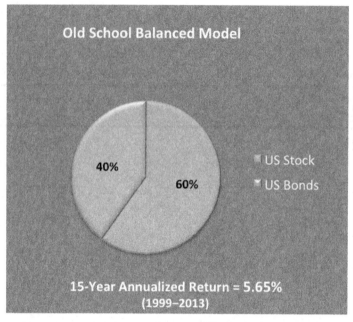
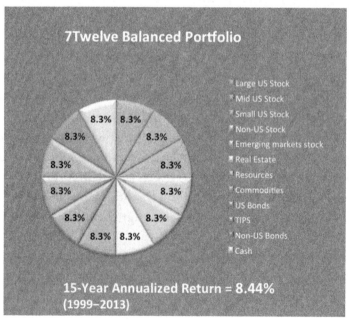

How would this 7Twelve portfolio have performed over a fifteen-year period (1999–2013) in comparison to the classic balanced portfolio and the stock market? The results are represented on the following chart.

7Twelve®: A Better Model

Calendar Year Total % Return (*Assuming annual rebalancing*)	7Twelve® Balanced Portfolio*	Vanguard Balanced Index	Vanguard 500 Index
1999	16.02	13.61	21.07
2000	6.77	-2.04	-9.06
2001	-1.66	-3.02	-12.02
2002	-0.78	-9.52	-22.14
2003	27.09	19.87	28.50
2004	17.76	9.33	10.74
2005	12.17	4.65	4.77
2006	15.15	11.02	15.64
2007	11.31	6.16	5.39
2008	-24.62	-22.21	-37.02
2009	24.90	20.05	26.49
2010	14.50	13.13	14.91
2011	-1.01	4.14	1.97
2012	10.85	11.32	15.83
2013	9.54	17.96	32.19
15-Year % Return (1999–2013)	8.44	5.65	4.58
15-Year Growth of $10,000	33,702	22,807	19,585

* Performance reflects the actual performance of twelve underlying exchange traded funds (ETFs.

Some observations worth noting:

1. The 7Twelve portfolio underperformed the S&P 500 in more than half of the years. However, its average annual return overall was dramatically higher (almost double). Again, trying to outperform "the market" every year is not a useful goal. However, achieving more consistent returns and reducing portfolio drawdown (2002, 2008) is a way to outperform over time. In Israelsen's own words, "One important rule: Negative returns are disproportionately more damaging to a portfolio than positive returns of the same size."
2. All three strategies above suffered declines in 2008. No matter which strategy you choose, you are better off not selling in a down year. If you do, you lose. Stick to your unemotional strategic game plan. However, the portfolio that suffers less of a drawdown is easier to stomach and more likely to outperform over time (when comparing portfolios of similar risk tolerance).
3. The 7Twelve portfolio referenced on the previous page used ETFs in its analysis. However, the instrument used to represent the asset class is not the determinant of returns. Israelsen has found similar results when using index funds and actively managed mutual funds. The key is asset classes used in specific ratios as opposed to the specific fund selection.
4. You can outperform conventional wisdom strategies!

The next chart expands our comparison between the 7Twelve portfolio and other portfolios over that same fifteen-year time frame. Most importantly, take note of the last portfolio.

Asset Allocation Risk and Return Spectrum – January 2014
Craig L. Israelsen, PhD
15-Year Period from 1999–2013
www.7TwelvePortfolio.com

Risk Level	Various Asset Allocation Models		15-Year Annualized Return (%) of Lump Sum Investment	15-Year Growth of $10,000 Lump Sum Investment*	Retirement Account Ending Balance** (see next page)
Very Conservative	100% Cash		2.35	14,174	98,984
Conservative	50% Cash 50% Bonds		3.78	17,458	151,452
Moderately Aggressive	60% US Stock 40% Bonds Traditional "Balanced" Fund		5.45	22,172	176,026
Moderately Aggressive	8.33% in 12 Different Asset Classes Diversified 7Twelve® Portfolio		8.44	33,702	438,457

Very Aggressive	100% US Stock		4.58	19,590	91,205
Crazy	Chasing Last Year's Best Performing Asset Class (from among 12)		0.66	11,043	43,294

* Ending account balance on December 31, 2013 assuming a lump sum investment of $10,000 on January 1, 1999 (15-year period).

** Ending account balance on December 31, 2013 in a retirement portfolio with a starting balance of $250,000 on January 1, 1999, 5% initial withdraw rate, 3% cost of living increase in the annual cash withdrawal. A total of 15 annual withdrawals totaling $232,486.

7Twelve® is a registered trademark belonging to Craig L. Israelsen.

What should be emphasized from this chart is the last portfolio, which appropriately has a picture of a dog chasing its tail. This represents a hypothetical investor who invests 100 percent of his or her portfolio in the best performing of the twelve funds/asset classes from the previous year. This is the investor who, like the dog chasing its tail, is chasing returns. As you can see, wanting to invest in the best performer, *what emotionally would feel good*, leads to almost no performance.

We don't want to be the investor chasing performance, so what is our defense against these emotional triggers? Systems! Systematically set up your allocation and systematically rebalance on an annual basis. The rebalancing will force you to redirect some of the profits from top performing asset classes into the cheaper ones. It is a forced buy low and sell high system. If left up to your own volition, are you likely to sell some from your top performers? Probably not.

Can we do better than buying and holding the classic portfolio of stocks and bonds? I believe so, and Professor Israelsen's work confirms this. Does this require countless hours of research and monitoring? No, it can be as simple as adding more diversification and rebalancing on a regular basis. The key for any system to work (including buy-and-hold) is to stick to it.

In addition to the 7Twelve portfolio offering us an unemotional system to follow and the chance for stronger returns, I believe it is also better equipped to face the potential challenges of inflationary and/or rising rate environments outlined earlier because of its added diversification. This is why I feel that for those with a moderate to moderately aggressive risk tolerance, the 7Twelve portfolio formula could be considered a core holding within a portfolio. This would also be an ideal portfolio strategy for a 401(k) or 403(b) account. The key to implementing this within your work-based retirement plan is that the menu of investment options in the plan has to be robust enough to offer all twelve fund types.

I don't encourage deviating from the system too much, but a minor tweak is feasible. For example, adding some floating rate bonds within the bond allocation in the face of rising rates might be prudent. The key is to keep the asset class percentages fixed and to rebalance to those percentages.

More drastic asset allocation changes, such as selling all stock and moving 100 percent into bonds or cash, is way too drastic. Making major asset allocation changes, being tactical, is best left up to the professional managers who have a proven track record of success. Now that you've been introduced to a better, more diversified balanced portfolio, the next chapter will explore tactical allocation portfolios.

For more information regarding the 7Twelve portfolio, consider visiting: www.7twelveportfolio.com

In Summary

- There are additional asset classes beyond stocks, bonds, and cash.
- There are additional money management strategies than just buy-and-hold that can play defense in addition to offense.
- Some of the best-run portfolios are college endowments, which utilize a lot of the aforementioned strategies.
- Until recently, many of these strategies were not available to the individual investor. Only large institutional or accredited investors had access to them.

What makes finding sources of uncorrelated returns so important? The answer is in two words: controlling risk. When you combine assets that don't correlate with each other in a portfolio, you get the average of all the returns but with less than the average risk of each investment taken separately. Low correlation puts the disco in diversification.

—Ben Stein and Phil DeMuth, *The Little Book of Alternative Investments*

CHAPTER 8

TACTICAL ASSET ALLOCATION

Questions: Knowing what you now know, would you want to own a broad basket of bonds in a rising rate environment? Wouldn't you agree that we need to consider the current environment we are in when deciding our asset allocation?

"Tactical asset allocation [TAA] is a dynamic strategy that actively adjusts a portfolio's strategic asset allocation [SAA] based on short-term market forecasts. Its objective is to systematically exploit inefficiencies or temporary imbalances in equilibrium values among different assets or sub-asset classes."

http://seekingalpha.com/article/97860-tactical-asset-allocation-part-i

This is the solution that we alluded to in our early discussion about mutual funds and their management goals. Instead of choosing a manager to just purchase a niche category of stocks or bonds, such as large caps or small caps, here we are hiring them to tactically manage the portfolio's asset allocation given the current environment at the time. After all, the asset classes that you are invested in determine most of your return. With tactical allocation, many managers are less concerned about choosing specific stocks or bonds that they think will outperform. Instead, they are more concerned with making macro calls on which asset classes to overweight (add more exposure to) and underweight (decrease exposure to) by often investing in indexes, ETFs, or mutual funds for those exposures.

For example, if the manager believes that we are heading into an inflationary environment, he or she might shift away from government bonds and into commodities. If the manager contends that rising rates are in the near future, he or she may proactively employ bond strategies with lower duration. Conversely, the traditional—Old World—asset allocation models are static in nature (unadapting), holding fixed percentages to asset classes no matter the environment they are in. Which sounds more appealing to you?

As a rule of thumb, tactical managers are much more risk aware. Many are more concerned with preserving assets and capital than with trying to swing for the fences one year only to strike out the next. Now, there is nothing wrong with an aggressive philosophy in a vacuum, but is that how common investors want their hard-earned money managed? There are casinos for that.

At the end of the day, all investors would love for their portfolios to always go up and never go down. The only philosophy that gives you *a shot* of accomplishing something remotely similar to this is outlined in the next three chapters. The buy-and-hold of a major stock index is guaranteed *not to* provide you with such results.

If you can get more consistent returns year after year and avoid major losses, you will grow your money more steadily over time. This will also better allow you, the investor, to stay invested and to not let the fear of a loss cause you to make an emotional decision to sell.

Many investors want fund managers to yield the highest return all the time. If the manager is receiving a management fee, he or she should be earning it through consistent outperformance. I would submit to you that such a goal is nearly impossible to live up to. Where I believe active managers can truly earn their fees is in the risk management or the downside protection from major bear markets. If you can sidestep much of those downdrafts, you can easily be outperforming over time. I would submit to you that helping you accomplish this is much more realistic, achievable, and is an incredibly valuable service.

Some examples of investments that follow this philosophy are to follow. What most of these strategies share in common are more consistent and less volatile returns than simply investing in the S&P 500 Index. They may underperform the index in strong bull markets, such as the one in the late 1990s, since they are all diversified and will not be 100 percent in stocks as the index is. On the flip side, they will most likely outperform the index in bear markets. This is partly due to diversification and partly due to tactical management and global macro calls.

The periodic table of asset classes that Craig Israelsen provided in chapter three showed the annual returns of various asset classes in recent years. This doesn't exhibit all of the options or asset classes available to a given manager, but it should give you an idea of the concept of how different asset classes move at different times throughout the economic cycles. These would be the types of choices that a given manager would be potentially adding and subtracting exposure to.

The key to tactical allocation is that it factors in the current and near-term market environment. In theory, a tactical manager will be constantly overweighting and underweighting these specific asset classes based on current market and economic conditions. Tactical allocation is not emotionally easy to implement for the undisciplined investor. It often requires one to sell asset classes that have run up and to buy asset classes that have been depressed. This strategy is best left to a proven money manager with a proven track record in both bull and bear markets.

Two observations on tactical management options:

1. It is less of a strategy of outperformance and more of a strategy of risk management and downside protection.

This in turn may lead to outperformance over time. In addition, I believe it is more aligned with the desires of common investors (risk-controlled growth), as opposed to index outperformance.
2. The financial services industry has promoted the value of mutual fund managers to be specific security selection (stock picking within a benchmark universe) rather than tactical management. Therefore, our menu of tactical managers with lengthy track records is (because it is rare) very slim.

In addition to being categorized as "tactical allocation" you will find many tactical fund options also labeled as "conservative, moderate, or world allocation" offerings within Morningstar, or any other fund filtering software. In layman's terms, we can consider them go-anywhere funds that have the ability to invest in any asset class of their choosing with the added flexibility to play stronger defense, which may involve selling a good portion of the portfolio or going to cash or another less risky asset class. It is worth repeating that these characteristics are not shared by the mandates of most funds. This style of management is very much akin to the premise behind hedge funds, in which there are fewer restrictions or constraints on the management of the portfolio. However, hedge funds aren't widely available for purchase, and they often carry hefty expenses. Therefore, we will concentrate on more accessible mutual fund options.

Chart Analysis

Before we analyze these various tactical recommendations, we need to understand one of the charts that we will be examining. It will help us distinguish the value of these strategies. What you have here is a representation of the classic relationship between risk and return represented by the following risk/return matrix. Profitability and return increase vertically, and the risk of the portfolio (standard deviation) increases to the right. The two axes are running through the S&P 500, as a measurement of comparison. This is what we are going to compare our portfolios to.

The first question is: Which quadrant do you want your portfolio to be in? A? B? C? D?

Which quadrant is the most appealing to you?

Quadrant A: Low risk, High return

Quadrant B: High risk, High return

Quadrant C: Low risk, Low return

Quadrant D: High risk, Low return

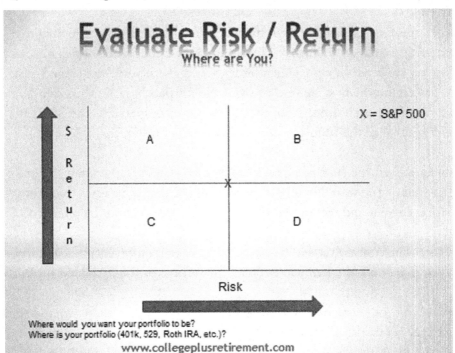

Quadrants B and C make conceptual sense. If I were to take more risk by moving to the right in the chart, I will most likely get a higher return over time by moving up the chart. Conversely, if I were to take less risk by moving to the left in the chart, I most likely will get less return over time by moving down on the chart. Therefore, when portfolios or individual investments show up in these quadrants, they can be viewed as acceptable, if the portfolio matches the investor's risk tolerance.

Quadrants D and A are a little bit different. Not only is quadrant D taking on more risk than the market, but it is also indicating less return. This is the worst of both worlds; it is portfolio hell. If the D quadrant stands for the devil portfolio, the A stands for the angel portfolio, or portfolio heaven. The A quadrant is the best of both worlds. It is less risky than the market, and it also has higher returns. This is where you would ideally love to be positioned.

Keep this relationship of risk/return familiar as you review the highlighted tactically managed strategies. The seven tactical mutual fund recommendations are listed in alphabetical order. Check with your brokerage house to determine the best share class available for purchase. In the examples, we will analyze statistics from the past decade compared to the S&P 500 Index, or since the fund's inception—whichever is longer.

*Sidenote: In the scattergraphs to follow, you will see the strategy name followed by the word "before." You can ignore this. This is used for comparing current and recommended portfolios, and it cannot be removed.

*Note: The common wisdom is that you can never outperform the market. Keep this in mind when you evaluate the returns of the following funds.

For each fund there are two charts. The top chart is the risk/return matrix with the previously discussed A, B, C, and D quadrants. The bottom chart is a graph of historical performance compared to the S&P 500 Index.

Tactical Asset Allocation

1. **BlackRock Global Allocation (MDLOX):** "The Fund seeks to provide high total investment return through a fully managed investment policy utilizing U.S. and foreign equity, debt and money market securities, the combination of which will be varied from time to time both with respect to types of securities and markets in response to changing market and economic trends." (Source: Blackrock.com)

   Here is a YouTube video on the fund: http://www.youtube.com/watch?feature=player_embedded&v=l1C7d2kzHz0#!.

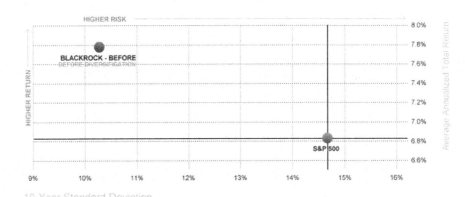

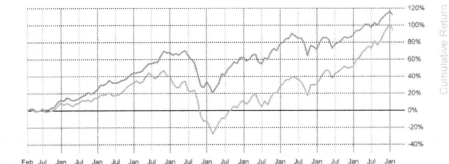

STATS: For the time period (shown above) of January 31, 2004 through January 31, 2014, the average annual return for MDLOX was 7.77 percent versus 6.83 percent for the S&P 500 Index. In addition, MDLOX exhibited a standard deviation (risk) measurement (the lower, the better) of 10.28 versus 14.67 for the index. Lastly, MDLOX achieved a cumulative return of 111.43 percent versus 93.68 percent for the index.

2. **FPA Crescent (FPACX):** Taken straight from their website, here are some poignant statements about the fund that are in perfect alignment with the theme of this book:
   - "The fund seeks to generate equity-like returns over the long-term, take less risk than the market, and avoid permanent impairment of capital.
   - We aim to protect capital first and to create long-term equity-like returns second. We cannot eliminate risk, but we conduct ourselves by hoping for the best, while preparing for the worst.
   - We invest our money alongside yours, and we act as stewards of our shared capital." (Source: fpa-funds.com)

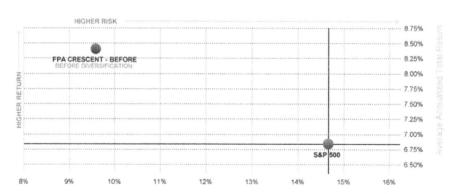

Tactical Asset Allocation

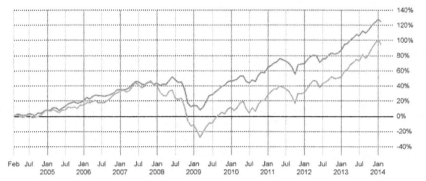

STATS: For the time period (shown above) of January 31, 2004 through January 31, 2014, the average annual return for FPACX was 8.40 percent versus 6.83 percent for the S&P 500 Index. In addition, FPACX exhibited a standard deviation (risk) measurement of (the lower the better) 9.59 versus 14.67 for the index. Lastly, FPACX achieved a cumulative return of 124 percent versus 93.68 percent for the index.

3. **GMO Benchmark Free Allocation (GBMFX):** Since you need at least $10 million to gain access to this fund, most investors will need to rely on purchasing the **Wells Fargo Advantage Absolute Return (WARDX)** fund, which invests 100 percent of the account in the GMO strategy. However, because the Wells Fargo option is relatively new and has a limited track record, we will use GMO's track record and Wells Fargo's description.

"The Wells Fargo Advantage Absolute Return Fund is a nontraditional fund that seeks positive total returns—with an emphasis on capital preservation—through tactical allocations to equity, bond, and alternative investments." (Source: wellsfargoadvantagefunds.com)

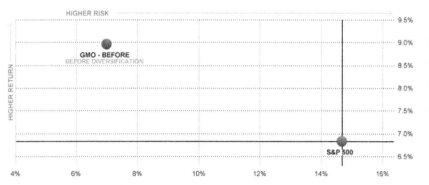

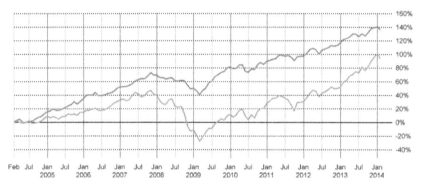

STATS: For the time period (shown above) of January 31, 2004 through January 31, 2014, the average annual return for GBMFX was 8.97 percent versus 6.83 percent for the S&P 500 Index. In addition, GBMFX exhibited a standard deviation (risk) measurement (the lower the better) of 6.99 versus 14.67 for the index. Lastly, GBMFX achieved a cumulative return of 136 percent versus 93.68 percent for the index.

4. **Intrepid Capital (ICMBX):** The talking points are straight from their website and clearly echo the premise of this chapter and this book:
    - "We invest our own money alongside the funds of our clients.

Tactical Asset Allocation

- We do not follow the herd on Wall Street.
- We typically are not correlated to benchmark indices because:
    - We have a concentrated portfolio consisting of our best ideas.
    - We do not attempt to match our sector weightings to benchmarks.
    - We are flexible and do not have cash limits."

(Source: intrepidcapitalfunds.com)

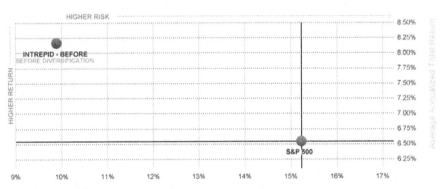

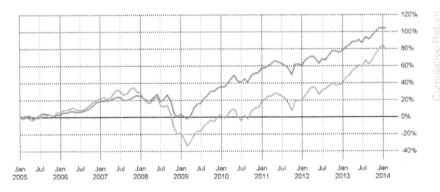

STATS: For the time period (shown above) of December 31, 2004 through January 31, 2014, the average annual return for ICMBX was 8.16 percent versus 6.55 percent for the S&P 500 Index. In addition, ICMBX exhibited a standard deviation (risk) measurement of (the lower the better) 9.90 versus 15.23 for the index. Lastly, ICMBX achieved a cumulative return of 103.93 percent versus 77.87 percent for the index.

5. **Ivy Asset Strategy (WASYX):** Ivy describes this fund as follows: "The fund may invest in any market that we believe offers a high probability of return or, alternatively, that provides a high degree of safety in uncertain times. Dependent on the outlook for the United States and global economies, we identify growth themes and then make top-down allocations among stocks, bonds, cash, precious metals, currency, and derivatives instruments. After determining allocations, we seek attractive opportunities within each market by focusing on issues in countries, sectors, and companies with strong cash flow and low balance-sheet leverage." (Source: Ivyfunds.com)

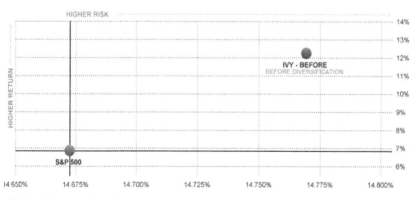

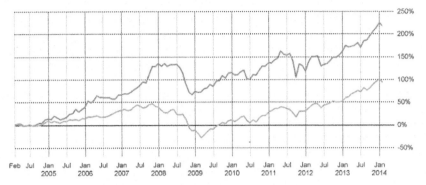

STATS: For the time period (shown above) of January 31, 2004 through January 31, 2014, the average annual return for WASYX was 12.25 percent versus 6.83 percent for the S&P 500 Index. In addition, WASYX exhibited a standard deviation (risk) measurement that was slightly higher than the index at 14.77 versus 14.67 for the index. Lastly, WASYX achieved a cumulative return of 217.61 percent versus 93.68 percent for the index.

6. **James Balanced: Golden Rainbow (GLRBX):** The investment objective as described by their fund fact sheet states: "The James Balanced: Golden Rainbow Fund seeks to provide total return through a combination of growth and income and preservation of capital in declining markets." In addition, it states a reassuring strategic philosophy they share regarding how they manage their bond positions: "The fixed income portion of the Fund's portfolio will usually consist primarily of U.S. government securities or high grade corporate bonds. When the Adviser believes that interest rates will fall, it may extend maturities in anticipation of capital appreciation in the bonds.

If the Adviser believes interest rates may rise, it will seek capital preservation through the purchase of shorter term bonds."

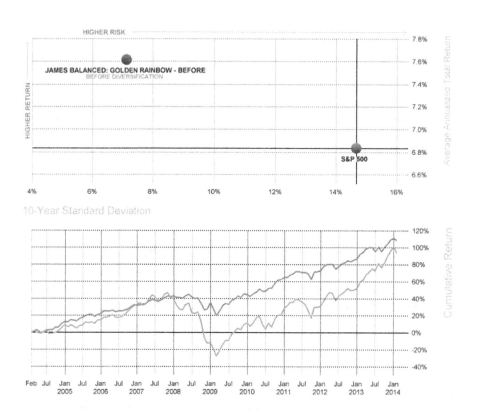

STATS: For the time period (shown above) of January 31, 2004 through January 31, 2014, the average annual return for GLRBX was 7.62 percent versus 6.83 percent for the S&P 500 Index. In addition, GLRBX exhibited a standard deviation (risk) measurement of (the lower the better) 7.12 versus 15.23 for the index. Lastly, GLRBX achieved a cumulative return of 108.34 percent versus 93.68 percent for the index

7. **Pimco All Asset All Authority (PAUDX):** Pimco describes this fund as "With its dynamic asset allocation approach, the fund targets solid real (after-inflation) returns from a global opportunity set of traditional and alternative asset classes. It can also use controlled amounts of leverage and short U.S. stocks. The resulting portfolio may help you protect purchasing power and pursue growth potential across a range of market environments." (Source: investments.pimco.com)

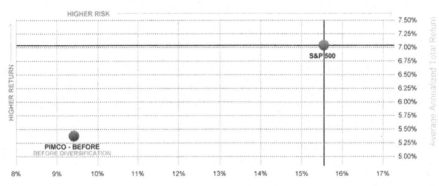

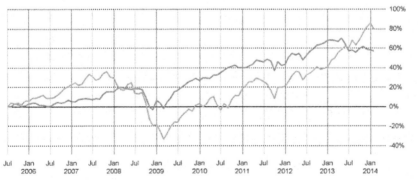

STATS: For the time period (shown above) of June 30, 2005 through January 31, 2014, the average annual return for PAUDX was 5.38 percent versus 7.04 percent for the S&P 500 Index. In addition, PAUDX exhibited a standard deviation (risk) measurement of (the lower the better) 9.42 versus 15.55 for the index. Lastly, PAUDX achieved a cumulative return of 56.80 percent versus 79.33 percent for the index.

Other noteworthy (tactical) considerations: American Independence MAR Tactical funds managed by Cougar Global (mutual fund versions of their strategies are brand new), Eaton Vance Global Macro Return (more concentrated on global bonds), First Eagle Global (more concentrated toward stocks), Invesco Balanced Risk Allocation (excellent strategy, but its inception was after 2008).

> **Note: Six out of seven options have outperformed the S&P 500 Index over their respective time frames. Six out of seven options have exhibited less risk than the S&P 500 Index over the same time periods.**

What all of these strategies have in common is the flexibility and freedom of the portfolio managers to move money to the asset classes and underlying investments that they believe warrant investment. This is contrary to most funds, which have to remain fully invested at all times and can only select their positions from a small subset of the investment universe.

These types of strategies may underperform the stock indexes in raging bull markets like the one in the late 1990s. However, the value is added in bear markets, when tactical managers are better able to position portfolios to play defense against major declines. Thus they will most likely outperform during bear markets. Less severe peaks and troughs lead to less turbulence and a smoother flight for the portfolio passengers.

*Note: Buying and holding a tactical strategy is not the same as buying and holding the market, as a tactical strategy will perform the buying and selling for you over time.

Since you have reached this point in the book, I encourage you to take this three-question questionnaire:

Investment Questionnaire

1. **Q: What would you like the goal of your portfolio to be?**

   Check the answer that best fits your philosophy.

   _____ Attempt to outperform a particular index (i.e., S&P 500 Index) on an annual basis.

   _____ Achieve more consistent annual returns with growth in up (bull) markets and provide above-average protection from major down (bear) markets.

2. **Q: Which set of performance numbers best represents how you would like your portfolio to perform in down (bear) and up (bull) markets?**

   Check the answer that best fits your philosophy.

	2008	2009
_____	-7.53 percent	18.98 percent
_____	-11.23 percent	20.65 percent

_____   -26.50 percent   20.33 percent
_____   -37.02 percent   26.49 percent

3. **Q: Which portfolio management strategy is the most appealing to you?**

Check the answer that best fits your philosophy.

_____ Buy–and–hold: choose a set portfolio and never adjust or make changes.

_____ Tactical management: consistently adjust portfolio factoring in the current market and economic environments.

Question 1. If you chose the first option, then you are of the mind-set of most of the mutual fund industry. As Vanguard acknowledges in the previously referenced paper, you are fighting an uphill battle. If that is your goal, the odds are that you will be a very frustrated investor. However, if you happen to find a strategy that can beat its index every year, please contact me!

Answer two is, in my opinion, more achievable and more in line with the true tolerance for risk of most investors. This desired outcome is tailor made for tactical asset allocation strategies.

Question 2. The first set of returns represents Pimco All Asset All Authority fund (PAUDX). The second set of returns represents GMO Benchmark Free III fund (GBMFX). The third set of returns represents Vanguard LifeStrategy Moderate Growth Inv (VSMGX), which is almost a perfect representation of the classic sixty–forty stock/bond portfolio, and the fourth set of returns represents the Vanguard 500 Index Inv (VFINX).

Thus if the first two sets of returns are more appealing to you, then you may want to hire a tactical manager. If the second two sets of returns are more appealing to you, then you may want to (try) a buy-and-hold strategy using Vanguard Index funds.

Question 3. See if your answer matches your desired results from the previous two questions.

Tactical Allocation 2.0

Some tactical managers will maneuver within a collection of asset classes, adding exposure to some and decreasing exposure to others. As rare as those managers are, the next group is even rarer. Tactical allocation 2.0 represents a management style that primarily deals with two asset classes, stocks and cash. On a regular basis these managers determine whether to be fully invested in the stock market, be 100 percent removed and sitting in cash (or short-term treasuries), or somewhere in the middle by utilizing ETFs. Tactical 2.0 managers have various systems for analyzing how much exposure to allocate to the market at any one particular time. This group is 180 degrees from the "typical" mutual funds outlined in our critique in chapter three.

Below are two management groups that provide offerings that follow this type of management style. They both follow the mantra of "win by not losing" and do not practice buy-and-hold.

1. **Forward Tactical Growth (FFTGX):**
   This strategy is a continuation of a former hedge fund that Broadmark Asset Management ran. The same manager is in place, and Forward Management LLC has created a separately managed account and mutual fund version of this strategy. In the words of Forward Management, "The Forward Tactical Growth Portfolio seeks to produce

above-average, risk-adjusted returns, in any market environment, while exhibiting less downside volatility than the S&P 500 Index."... "The portfolio is designed to help investors side-step market downturns, while participating in its growth via the continuous and active management of portfolio market exposure. The portfolio seeks to manage risk and enhance alpha with the flexibility to take a long, short or neutral view on the market."

The strategy usually adds and decreases stock exposure, depending on the current market valuations, sentiment readings, monetary policy, and market trends. At times the mutual fund managers could even be 100 percent in cash or even bet against the market (via shorting). This flexibility has allowed the Broadmark management team to compile an impressive long-term risk-controlled track record. Since the hedge fund performance is not public information, I cannot publish it here. However, I will say that it provided terrific downside protection (in fact, actually positive) in the bear markets affiliated with the years 2002 and 2008.

A video outlining Broadmark's philosophy can be found here: http://www.morningstar.com/advisor/v/59279037/looking-to-win-by-not-losing.htm?advt=true

http://video.foxbusiness.com/v/1795565453001/.

You can find out more information on this management team here: http://www.forwardinvesting.com/.

2. **Good Harbor US Tactical Core (GHUAX, GHUCX, GHUIX):**

Good Harbor runs a fund that is similar to Forward Tactical Growth, whereby this strategy can be extremely defensive or very aggressive. Good Harbor describes their strategy like this: "The underlying premise of the Good Harbor tactical model is that equity prices are driven by changes in investor risk premiums and that these premiums vary with the business cycle. By gauging a combination of momentum measures, economic data and yield curve dynamics, the model seeks to assess changes in risk premiums in order to participate in equities during rallies and move defensively to bonds when weaker market conditions are anticipated."

They too have produced excellent, consistent returns:

2003: 33.12% (April 30–December 31)

2004: 14.52%

2005: -3.81%

2006: 10.68%

2007: -.36%

2008: -.07%

2009: 47.27%

2010: 12.92%

2011: 12.73%

2012: 5.77%

2013: 24.60%

A $1,000 investment in this strategy at inception would have grown to $3,993 versus $2,508 for the S&P 500 over that time frame. In other words, your portfolio would be over 37 percent higher than if you bought and held the S&P 500. (Source: Good Harbor)

*Note: We have taken all numbers from Good Harbor's website. Their fact sheet can be found here: http://www.goodharborfinancial.com/strategies/strategy.pl?S=Tactical%20Core

In 2013, they launched a mutual fund version of this strategy (ticker symbols above).

Interestingly, investors look at the year-by-year returns and compare them to a broad index. Many conventional thinking investors would be unhappy that these two funds did not beat the index every year, but this is not our goal. Again, don't fall into that portfolio manager's trap of comparing everything to the index on short timetables. Remember, if your fund exhibits a -35 percent decline in 2008, compared with the -37 percent decline for the S&P 500, although it is a victory to the industry, it isn't to you or me. Look at Good Harbor's performance in 2007 and 2008. As you can see, there was no growth. Are you unhappy with that? Many investors may instinctually say yes, but should they? In those two years Good Harbor exhibited risk control via tactical management. Again, the goal isn't to outperform an index every year. The goal is to try to achieve more consistent returns by sidestepping major declines. The goal is to win by not losing. It is this philosophy that allows the strategy after a decade to be over 37 percent higher than the market.

3. **Good Harbor Tactical Equity Income (GHTAX, GHTCX, GHTIX):**

This is a unique blend of themes mentioned in previous chapters. Good Harbor says that the strategy "invests in companies whose revenues and earnings are derived from tangible assets, such as Real Estate Investment Trusts (REITs), Master Limited Partnerships (MLPs), basic materials, and energy-related companies. These types of companies generally demonstrate stable cash flows, deliver above-average yields, and hold potential for modest growth accompanied by a margin of safety. The strategy takes positions in these through direct ownership of stocks, which are supplemented with equity options. During less favorable environments or when attractive investment opportunities are limited, the strategy has the flexibility to invest in cash or short-duration US treasuries."

The results are eye-popping, and they speak for themselves:

2001: 30.83%

2002: 11.13%

2003: 40.94%

2004: 14.31%

2005: 21.68%

2006: 10.41%

2007: -2.34%

2008: .02%

2009: 123.47%

2010: 18.43%

2011: -7.89%

2012: 11.74%

2013: 9.22%

A $1,000 investment in this strategy at inception would have grown to $9,146 versus $1,805 for the S&P 500 over that time frame. In other words, your portfolio would be over 80 percent higher than if you bought and held the S&P 500. (Source: Good Harbor)

*Note: We have taken all numbers from Good Harbor's website. Their fact sheet can be found here: http://www.goodharborfinancial.com/strategies/strategy.pl?S=Tactical%20Equity

In 2013, Good Harbor launched a mutual fund version of this strategy (tickers symbols above).

My prediction: in the next decade you will see a plethora of new strategies that will be chasing the success and mirroring the management styles of the funds listed in this chapter.

The idea of winning by not losing and not remaining fully invested in stocks at all times exhibited by these strategies leads us to the next chapter, in which we identify major trends in the market. Unlike the current chapter, which involves delegating all investment decisions, the next chapter identifies ways in which you can become more proactive with your portfolio, if it suits you to do so.

How can you possibly do your asset allocation without looking at the market values of the asset classes out there today? That's probably the most valuable information you can get as to the future prospects of those asset classes, and what astounds me is the fact that many people—many of them very sophisticated—do asset allocation without even checking to see what the relative values of the outstanding shares in, say, European securities, US securities, emerging markets, etc., are.

—Bill Sharpe, interview at IndexUniverse.com, 2008

CHAPTER 9

TREND ANALYSIS: WINNING BY NOT LOSING

Question: What if I could show you a way to avoid the next major bear market? Would you be interested?

If you still believe in buy-and-hold, this chapter will really challenge your faith.

Note: The ideas expressed in this chapter may not be appropriate for every investor. Implementing a trend-following strategy takes the highest level of discipline, and it is contrary to typical behavioral tendencies (often buying when uncomfortable and selling when comfortable).

As outlined in chapter two, the issue with the herd mentality is that the common investors are typically at the tail end of the herd. Trend analysis allows us to be ahead of the majority of the herd with major movements, but more importantly not wind up last. This can only be accomplished when emotions are removed from our investment decisions. We have to react to data rather than instincts. Therefore, I am fully aware that this can be more difficult to implement than most strategies (more personal management, less delegation), but as you will find, there are major benefits. This strategy allows you to proactively play both offense and defense to grow and protect your nest egg. Moreover, from an emotional standpoint, this will alleviate much of those painful feelings of helplessness and inaction often experienced during bear market downturns.

I am in favor of low-cost investing through index mutual funds. However, as we outlined in the previous chapter, a stock index fund is passive and will not implement tactical allocation management on your behalf. More importantly, it won't provide you any cushion from major drawdowns like the one in 2002 or 2008. In fact, you are *guaranteed not to avoid it*. This chapter teaches you not how to be like a helpless index fund but rather introduces a proactive way to use indexing (via ETFs) as your personal steering wheel to more efficiently navigate the markets. Again, this is less about outpacing the market each and every year, which is virtually impossible. Instead, it is about knowing when to sidestep major declines and thereby win by not losing.

Conventional Wisdom: It is **time in the market—not the timing of the market**—that is the key driver to healthy performance numbers. Proponents of buy-and-hold investing tout the importance of always staying in the market. Their mantra is if you miss the best days, you will miss most of the potential returns. In other words, the *only* way to avoid underperformance is to always be invested.

Unconventional Wisdom: Neil R. Peplinski of Good Harbor Financial Inc. outlines unconventional wisdom in his paper "Active Investment Management and Time-Varying Investor Risk Premium." He points out that being tactful in the market can provide major benefits over buy-and-hold investing.

Peplinski analyzed the market from 1981 to 2009 and put this theory to the test with an added wrinkle. He asked what the results would look like if an investor did one of three things: 1) remained in the market 100 percent of the time, 2) missed the ten best days, or 3) missed the ten worst days.

Being fully invested throughout that time frame, the value of $1,000 invested in 1981 would have grown to $6,378. Missing the ten best days proved conventional wisdom to be true where $1,000 would have only grown to $3,076. However, if an investor missed the ten worst days, his or her $1,000 would have grown to $16,595. This bigger differential emphasizes the importance of being aware of risk and that avoiding major market declines actually yielded the best results *by far*. Therefore, it wasn't missing the best days that hurt investor returns the most (as conventional wisdom preaches), but rather it was *not* missing the worst days!

Further Evidence

An analysis by Paul Gire that appeared in the *Journal of Financial Planning* researched what happens when investors miss the best days, the worst days, and both (best and worst) days in the market. Gire found that for the fifteen-year period from 1984 to 1998 (a bull market), the **Dow averaged 17.89 percent** per year. Missing the ten best days reduced that average return to *14.24 percent*, but missing the worst ten days resulted in average annual returns of *24.17 percent*. Interestingly, if an investor missed the ten best and worst days, his or her average annual return was *20.31 percent*, which was still higher than the buy-and-hold return, thus proving that conventional wisdom on this issue is wrong. You can miss the best days and still achieve marketlike returns as long as you miss the worst days as well.

Additional data from the study can be found below:

# Of Trading Days Missed	Best	Worst	Both
10 days	14.24%	24.17%	20.31%
20 days	11.99%	27.04%	20.68%
30 days	10.01%	29.45%	20.80%
40 days	8.23%	31.66%	20.87%

Source: http://www.onefpa.org/journal/Pages/Missing%20the%20Ten%20Best.aspx

Therefore, the management of downside risk is equally as important as the management of positive returns! In other words, **to win the game, playing defense is equally as important as playing offense**. Anyone who has participated in sports can probably relate to this concept.

Moreover, this fits with what I believe is more in line with what the average investor is looking for: downside protection and more consistent returns. Many investors when faced with a major bear market are not interested in the prescription of inaction that Wall Street is selling. In the words of Jack Bogle, "Don't do something, Just stand there."

http://blogs.marketwatch.com/thetell/2014/02/03/jack-bogles-market-advice-dont-do-something-just-stand-there/

These "win without losing" approaches are appealing partially because of the potential to avoid the huge drawdowns and partially because of what is required in the aftermath. If an investor's portfolio is down 10 percent, he or she needs to then gain a little over 11 percent to get back to even. If the portfolio is down 20 percent, the investor needs to gain 25 percent. If the investor is down 50 percent, like many people were in 2008, he or she needs to gain 100 percent to get back to even.

A quick visual to aid your understanding:

Portfolio Value:	$100,000
Decline of 50 percent:	$50,000
An increase of 50 percent from there:	$75,000
An increase of 100 percent from there:	$100,000

> "One important rule: Negative returns are disproportionately more damaging to a portfolio than positive returns of the same size." —Craig L. Israelsen, developer of the 7Twelve portfolio

Counter to the industry's advice of always being invested in the market, some people might be willing to sacrifice some periods of growth (always being in the market) if they knew there was a way to help avoid most of the major drawdowns. The $64,000 question is: Is there a way to consistently avoid these major drawdowns?

My Introduction into Trend Following

As an avid reader of investment books, magazines, and newsletters, I was always looking to learn new ways to identify and select better investments. It wasn't too long before I began to read *Investor's Business Daily*, a popular daily newspaper written for individual investors. *IBD* is similar to the *Wall Street Journal* in that it reports on current news items and has an opinion section. However, it is unlike the *WSJ* in that it provides readers with a direction call in the markets. More specifically, it tells you whether we are in a bull or bear market. The paper stresses the importance of being on the right side of the market if you want to better manage your portfolio. This was a totally new concept to me. I had never heard of this theory when I was reading *A Random Walk Down Wall Street* in college or when I was in my training program and starting my career. One would assume that if *IBD*'s philosophy held any weight, it would be taught within the prestigious halls of higher education or within the walls of a Fortune 500 investment firm...but no. In addition, perhaps like you, I initially assumed that good stock pickers would excel in any market because of their keen investment selection and the companies they chose, irrespective of which direction the market went. Well, according to *IBD*, that isn't necessarily true either as **approximately 75 percent of all stocks move with their primary market.**

William J. O'Neil, the founder of *IBD*, is the author of many books, and he is well known for his "CAN SLIM" methodology for picking winning stocks. A major premise to the strategy is that you don't want to buy cheap stocks and hope that people eventually recognize their value.

Rather, he recommends buying stocks that have already begun appreciating. These are market-leading companies with accelerated earnings and price momentum (trending up). We as humans in society are so programed to get the cheapest price available, the best deal, buy-low-and-sell-high, etc. It is certainly a splash of water in the face to purchase stocks that aren't at their cheapest price—that have already begun to rise. If this is true, this goes against everything I have been taught.

The American Association for Individual Investors, which anyone can join for a small annual fee, hosts a website: www.aaii.com. Among other things, this website has unique stock filters that mimic some of the same methodologies used by some of the best investing minds in our time. For example, along with William O'Neil's CAN SLIM methodology, you can filter for stocks that would pass the screens for Warren Buffet, Benjamin Graham, Joel Greenblatt, Peter Lynch, and over sixty other investing legends. In the unhip world of analytical stock analysis, I think you can agree with me: that is pretty cool!

Not only does AAII provide screening capabilities, but they have also been tracking the performance of these portfolios for years. We have two interesting observational notes. AAII claims 94 percent of AAII stock screens outpace the market (so much for that "Random Walk" theory). Also, with over sixty of the best strategies for selecting stocks, O'Neil's CAN SLIM is always near the top in historical track record performance. This further confirms that O'Neil and *Investor's Business Daily*'s process and philosophy are sound. You can review performance numbers here: http://www.aaii.com/stock-screens/performance.

CAN SLIM is an acronym to help investors remember what to look for in companies before they purchase a stock. Much of this process requires some financial literacy, and it is best understood by reading *IBD* or one of O'Neil's books. I will explain this process briefly to provide some context. The "C" stands for "current quarterly earnings per share," which O'Neil recommends should be 18 percent or higher. The "A" stands for "annual earnings increases." This requires significant growth for each of the last three years and a return on equity of 17 percent or more. The "N" stands for "new products, new management, and new highs," again the last of which is counterintuitive to most investors. The "S" stands for "supply and demand." This requires big volume increases when a stock begins to move upward. The "L" stands for "leader" or "laggard." Investors want industry leaders. The "I" stands for "institutional sponsorship." They want it to be apparent that large institutions (pensions, mutual funds, etc.) are purchasing the stock. This brings us to the point of this section. Perhaps the most important letter in the acronym is the final letter.

The "M" in CAN SLIM stands for "market direction." Investors want to know whether the market is trending up or down (bull or bear). This will determine if you win big or lose big. I found this fascinating. After all the hard work of filtering all those company specifics to find appropriate stocks, it may all just come down to the direction of the market. The expertise you exhibited in finding the best companies for purchase might have been a fruitless exercise when confronted with the headwinds of a new bear market. This premise applies to all those mutual fund managers you have in your accounts as well. It helps explain why in major declines even the best mutual fund managers cannot avoid the declines amid the currents of a bear market.

To quote Mr. O'Neil himself, "You can be right on every one of the factors in the first six chapters" (which identified the first six letters/filter characteristics in CAN SLIM), "but if you're wrong about the direction of the general market, three out of four of your stocks will plummet with the market averages, and you will certainly lose money big time, as many people did in 2000."

Again, when the tides go out, all of the boats sink.

If approximately 75 percent of stocks will be influenced by the powerful force of the market direction, having an accurate read on the current market can prove invaluable. Some resources that may help you determine the direction of the tides are listed below.

> **Resources for Market Calls (in addition to *IBD*)**
> - **Market Edge:** Provides a market direction call available through their subscription service. It has an impressive track record (www.stkwtch.com/MarketEdge/ctisummary.htm), and you can research stats by signing up for a free trial or by visiting this website: www.marketedge.com
> - **The Dow Theory:** Provides a big-picture market call. It is a slow-moving indicator that does not change very often (slow moving). It is outlined in more detail at the end of this chapter. You can get an updated market call here: dowtheorybook.com
> - **VectorVest:** Provides a market-timing indicator that they claim has "never failed to signal a major up or down trend in the market." They encourage getting aggressive during up calls and defensive during down calls. They label this strategy "riding the wave." A chart of their calls goes back over a decade, and you can view it here: www.vectorvest.com/research/ridingthewave.aspx
> - **Wishing Wealth Blog:** Provides daily updates for Professor Dr. Eric Wish's proprietary buy and sell indicator (known as the GMI signal). The blog can be followed here: wishingwealthblog.com

Further validation that momentum in the market plays a major role in portfolio performance can be found in the 2011 paper produced by famous economists Eugene Fama, the father of the efficient market hypothesis, and Kenneth French. The duo is best known for their three-factor model, which emphasizes ownership of stocks over T-bills, value over growth stocks, and small companies over large companies as a model for outperformance. However, in a recent paper entitled "Size, Value, and Momentum in International Stock Returns," they stated that their three-factor model was not able to explain the effect that momentum has on investment performance. In analyzing North America, Europe, Japan, and Asia Pacific markets, they state, "Except for Japan, there is return momentum everywhere."

The aforementioned efficient market hypothesis again defined by Investopedia: "An investment theory that states it is impossible to 'beat the market' because stock market efficiency causes existing share prices to always incorporate and reflect all relevant information. According to the EMH, stocks always trade at their fair value on stock exchanges, making it impossible for investors to either purchase undervalued stocks or sell stocks for inflated prices. As such, it should be impossible to outperform the overall market through expert stock selection or market timing, and that the only way an investor can possibly obtain higher returns is by purchasing riskier investments."

Therefore, the hypothesis is stating that an investor cannot achieve market-like performance by trading in and out of the market. The only possible way to achieve better returns is to take on more risk. **Here is the irony:** even the inventor of the hypothesis is acknowledging a new market phenomenon (momentum). We intend to exploit this and actually prove that trading in and out of the market not only can achieve market-like returns, and here is the key, but may also do so with *less risk*!

What causes the momentum or trends in markets? This hasn't been entirely clear. Perhaps behavioral psychology is again rearing its head via herd mentality. Nobody has yet been able to pinpoint it. However, as the historical returns of managed futures strategies (which trades on trends) and academics such as French and Fama acknowledging the impact of momentum on returns, and the success of *Investor's Business Daily*'s CANSLIM model (just to name a few reference points), the conclusion we may make is that it most certainly exists. The next question should then be how can we incorporate this market trait within our investment portfolios?

Trend Strategy Number 1: Moving Averages

With hindsight being twenty-twenty, wouldn't it have been nice to have had an indicator that signaled you to exit the markets in late 2007? Only to then signal you to reenter in the spring of 2009, a time when almost no one was eager to enter the market? Could there be a simple way for the average investor to have done just that? It is possible. This approach is best known as moving average trend-following.

Here is a visual example. Let's take a look back at a five-year snapshot of the S&P 500 Index:

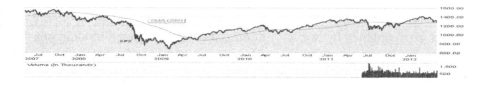

The thick line represents the S&P 500, and the thin line is the two-hundred-day simple moving average. Do you see where the thick line (the market) crossed below the thin line in the winter of 2007 (moving average = trend)? Do you see where it crossed above in the late spring of 2009? These crossover points are examples of common indicators that investors use in following trends.

> A moving average is simply a mean (average) number of the price of any investment over a specific amount of time and thus the trend. The two-hundred-day moving average referenced above expresses the average price of the S&P 500 over the past two hundred trading days.

If you think about just the past fifteen years, wouldn't you agree that the market moves in major trends over time? What did the market do in the late 1990s? It was a bull market. What did it do in the early 2000s? It was a bear market. What did the market do in the middle of the 2000s? It was a bull market. And so on. Therefore, if we had an unemotional gauge to tell us when to step on the gas or break with our portfolio, we might be able to take advantage of the majority of the move in a rising market, and we also might miss the majority of the move in a declining market.

Some may argue that it is hypocritical to espouse the virtues of such a strategy because it sounds a lot like market timing. However, the primary difference between trend-following and what most people think of as market timing is guesswork. Bogle hinted at this. This type of discipline we are discussing is unemotional. In fact, by following this methodology, you have better odds of not falling victim to the behavioral tendencies that have proven to lead to poor performance, and it requires zero guesswork.

Market Timing *often* involves:
- Attempting to pick market tops and bottoms
- Analyzing and reacting to current news and economic data
- Following gut or hunch

Trend Analysis *never* involves:
- Calling a market top or bottom
- Basing investment decisions on current news or economic data
- Emotional decisions

I fully acknowledge the splitting of hairs I am doing here. But trend analysis is very unique, and it does need its own individual characterization. The trouble is that doesn't exist currently. It is analogous to some activities being questionably labelled a sport (e.g., billiards, bowling, poker, etc.). As the old SAT questions were structured: Billiards is to Sports and Trend Trading is to Market Timing. In other words, it is, but it is also different.

The most traditional assumption of market timers is that they are trying to pick market tops and bottoms. I agree that this type of strategy is nearly impossible to do on a consistent basis. Interestingly enough, trend-following doesn't try to do that. In fact, it is *guaranteed to never call a market top or bottom.* Because we are utilizing mathematical averages no matter the time length, this strategy ensures that you will never exit at the top or enter at the exact bottom. However, it does provide you the opportunity to take advantage of the majority of a rising market and to miss the majority of a falling market. This is the magic formula that provides you with the opportunity to outpace a buy-and-hold strategy over time.

What are some simple trend indicators to follow?

1: You have a choice between an SMA or EMA (simple moving average or an exponential moving average). They are very similar. The major difference is that the exponential moving average gives more mathematical weight to more recent data points. They both work; it just comes down to personal preference.

> For a clearer explanation, you can watch a short video here: http://www.investopedia.com/video/play/SMA-versus-EMA.

2: You have a choice between time frames (look backs) of almost any length, the most popular being: fifty-day moving average, one hundred-day moving average, two hundred-day moving average. Note the two hundred-day is similar to the ten-month moving average, since there are five trading days per week and it takes forty weeks (ten months) to equal two hundred days.

The major issue with the time frame you select is the number of trades that you will have to make. I highly recommend a longer time horizon for a moving average to follow. You might choose a ten-month or twelve-month moving average. When you select a much shorter time frame than these options, you have to be much more attentive by doing more tracking and trading. Whether this produces better results over long periods of time is debatable. Our goal with this strategy is not to become day traders and sit in front of computer screens analyzing charts all day. **Our goal, rather, is to sidestep major bear markets and live our lives in the process.**

> **Recommendation: Use monthly indicators, not daily.**
>
> Chris Greene, CFA, is cofounder of ETFreplay.com Inc., a website with extensive backtesting capabilities for ETF quantitative methodologies. Having researched these types of strategies, he offers some valuable insight, "It is true across relative strength and ratio moving average backtesting, trying to stop losses too quickly and not giving trades some time and room to work generally hurts returns materially over the long run. Sometimes we buy things and for a few days you are really regretting it, but your discipline to only update at month-end forces you to give it some room. Sometimes the security comes back and finishes flat or slightly up, you hold, and then it surges up the next month. Had you taken the loss after the first few days, you would not only have a loss but you may not have the psychological power to get back in at a higher price and participate in the rally."

Let's examine some data and provide some historical perspective on how such strategies might have performed in the past.

One of the most useful websites for tracking various quantitative strategies is www.dark-liquidity.com. There is a wealth of information on this site and registration is free. You will be able to follow and research many sophisticated and intricate methodologies, along with simple and easy-to-follow strategies. For the purpose of this book, we will remain focused on systems that are easy to understand and quickly implemented. Therefore, we will stick to the popular two hundred-day simple and exponential moving averages.

On dark liquidity's website you can find graphs that compare the risk and return behavior of buy-and-hold portfolios versus following a two hundred-day simple moving average strategy. Of particular interest is the time frame known as "The Lost Decade," which was a frustrating time for buy-and-hold investors. Today's technology allows us to look back with hindsight and evaluate different and potentially better strategies. As we all know, history repeats itself and if we encounter another lost decade in the future, we want to be prepared and ready.

S&P 500 Index

Trade History: Buy $10,000 of SPY on January 3, 2001 at the market open price and sell on December 31, 2010 at the market closing price.

Trend Analysis: Winning by Not Losing

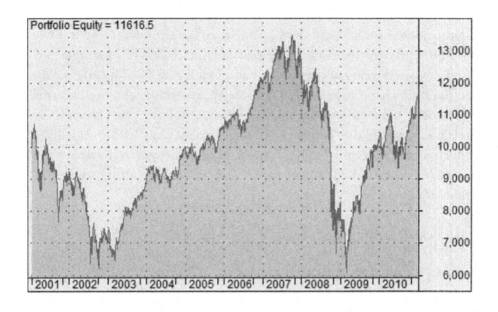

Graphically, this represents the roller coaster ride that a buy-and-hold investor would have experienced in order to grow his or her $10,000 investment to $11,616.50 over this decade.

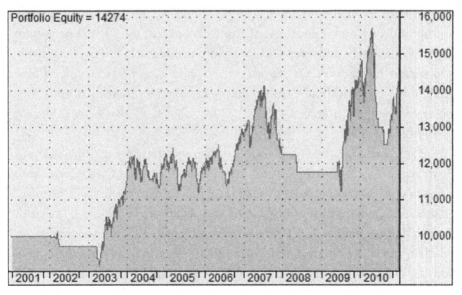

Graphically, this represents the path that an investor would have taken with $10,000 over that same time period while following a simple two hundred-day moving average entry and exit strategy. Not only would the portfolio have experienced greater appreciation, but the investor also would have experienced less downside volatility in the process (i.e., lower risk, higher returns). Notice the plateaus (flat lines) that are reflected in the graph. These are time periods of inactivity where the model would have had you sitting in cash patiently waiting to reenter the market.

Rhetorical question: Which graph is more appealing to you?

Nasdaq QQQ: The Real Lost Decade

If analyzing the S&P 500 over a decade wasn't enough to persuade you of the value of moving averages, my money is on the fact that the history of the Nasdaq Index might. One of the earliest ETFs ever created was designed to track the Nasdaq market (back in 1999), which is the PowerShares Nasdaq-100 Index (QQQ). Due to the Nasdaq's dramatic run-up and downturn courtesy of the tech bubble, QQQ investors who invested late in the bull run had to endure a traumatic roller coaster ride (graphically represented on the next chart). This is a great example of how challenging buy-and-hold can be when you have less than fortuitous timing as to when you invested.

I fully acknowledge that I am shooting fish in a barrel with this analysis. However, I use this example for a few reasons: 1) to emphasize how long it can take for some markets to recover from painful declines, 2) to offer further evidence that following a trend can yield better results, 3) to offer those who purchased QQQ in late 1999 and early 2000 a proactive strategy that may allow them to feel confident in eventually exiting their position for better opportunities. You don't have to be emotionally married to any one position if you have an unemotional system to help you make decisions.

Utilizing ETFReplay.com for backtesting capability, I ran a two hundred-day moving average backtest for the Nasdaq market (ticker: QQQ) going back to the earliest date available on ETFReplay.com (January 3, 2000).

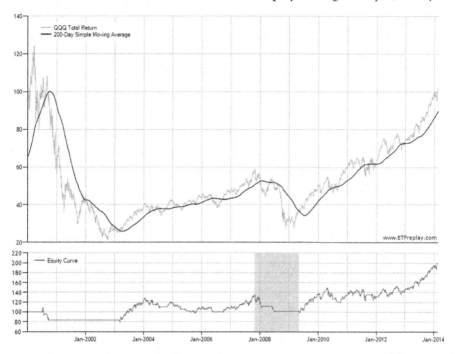

The thicker jagged line is the Nasdaq market and the thin line represents the two hundred-day moving average indicator. Again, the graph signifies buying or selling the Nasdaq Index on a monthly basis given whether the price of QQQ was above (buy) or below (sell) its moving average (or trend).

*Note: The bottom chart represents the growth of the moving average strategy portfolio.

	Buy and Hold	Moving Average Strategy
Total gain:	3.2%	100.1%
Largest drawdown:	83%	28.5%

In sum, the buy-and-hold investor after fourteen years just broke even. Meanwhile the systematic trend follower doubled his or her money.

A More Historical Perspective of Trend-Following

In ETF guru Tom Lydon's book *The ETF Trend-Following Playbook*, he references a similar study that Werner E. Keller (www.kellerpartners.com) performed, providing us with an expanded historical context. Keller analyzed how the two hundred-day *exponential moving average strategy* would have performed versus the S&P 500 buy-and-hold strategy. He examined two forty-year time periods: 1970–2008 and 1930–1970. They assumed a *2 percent cash return* when the market was below the two-hundred-day *EMA*.

A $100,000 investment in the S&P 500 in 1970 in a buy-and-hold strategy would have grown to $980,200 by 2008. Meanwhile, a $100,000 investment in 1970 in the S&P 500 utilizing a two hundred-day EMA strategy would have grown to $1,776,000. In addition, the largest drawdown (peak to trough) on the buy-and-hold strategy was -50.4 percent, while it was only -18.8 percent for the two hundred-day EMA portfolio. Therefore, the trend-following strategy would have allowed an investor to increase his or her return and to do so with less risk!

It is nice that we can apply these results to recent time periods, but would they have worked in the previous forty years (1930–1970) as well? Well, Keller calculated that a $100,000 portfolio that was invested in a buy-and-hold strategy in 1930 would have grown to $436,000 by 1970. Meanwhile, a $100,000 investment in 1930 in the S&P 500 utilizing a two hundred-day EMA strategy would have grown to $1,345,000. In addition, the largest drawdown on the buy-and-hold strategy was -71.6 percent, while it was only -35.1 percent for the two hundred-day EMA portfolio. In sum, less risk, higher return, and more in line with the most investors' risk tolerance (less drawdown).

You can follow the outlook of Keller Partners via their weekly blog at: http://www.kellerpartners.com/category/blog/.

Even More Historical Perspective Incorporating Different Time Frames

Would this strategy work with different moving averages? Tom Gleason analyzed this in his book *How To Invest If You Can't Afford To Lose*. Gleason ran various scenarios for simple moving averages compared to buy-and-hold over various *SMA time frames* (ten-month, twelve-month, fourteen-month, and sixteen-month SMAs) between 1952 and 2010. He assumed that he was invested in the S&P 500 when the market crossed above the corresponding simple moving averages and out of the market in cash when it crossed below its corresponding SMAs.

Assumption 1: Since the average money market rate during that time frame was 4.8 percent, Gleason assumed that *his money earned 4 percent while in cash*, when it was removed from the market. *Note: this amount may seem high now, but it wasn't too long ago that high-yield money market accounts advertised similar rates.

Assumption 2: Gleason's calculations used the S&P 500 Index without dividends.

Assumption 3: The entry dates for the various backtesting strategies differs for each moving average model, depending on when it initially triggered, hence the different buy-and-hold ending values.

Assumption 4: Ten thousand dollars is the starting value for both buy-and-hold and for the moving average models.

His results are as follows:

S&P 500: 1952 to 2010				
MA Cycle:	**10**	**12**	**14**	**16**
Buy & Hold:	$562,062	$532,725	$527,697	$538,977
Model:	$1,082,193	$1,310,572	$1,053,391	$1,204,694
Percent Better:	193%	246%	200%	224%
# of Trades:	43	33	28	27
Percent Success:	65%	70%	79%	81%
Median Gain:	14.67%	17.69%	19.69%	15.63%
Median Loss:	-4.66%	-4.38%	-4.18%	-3.80%
Time Invested:	68%	70%	71%	71%

Definitions

MA Cycle: Monthly moving average indicator used.

Buy-and-Hold: Growth of $10,000 initial investment using a buy-and-hold strategy.

Model: Growth of $10,000 initial investment using corresponding monthly moving average entry and exit strategy.

Percent Better: Percent better the model was over buy-and-hold.

# of Trades: The number of buy/sell transactions over the time period.

Percent Success: The percentage of trades that made money.

Median Gain: The median gain of the winning trades.

Median Loss: The median loss of the losing trades.

Time Invested: The amount of time the model was invested in the market.

Across all time frames, Gleason found dramatically better performance and less downside risk from the moving average models than buy-and-hold. Is every trade successful? Nope. However, the average gains are a lot higher than the average losses. Therefore, **keep your losses small and let your gains run.**

Moving average strategies are not guaranteed to outperform the market all the time. However, they will help you identify and potentially sidestep major bear markets. This is the disconnect between Main Street and Wall Street. To use an analogy, Wall Street is like an offense-obsessed home run-hitting baseball team. Their goal is to produce the highest returns every year (every inning) and think you should be of the same mind-set. Brushed off is the fact that their pitcher just gave up ten runs in the third inning (one bad bear market). What is overlooked when it comes to individual investors is that one bad inning can cost them the game (or successful retirement). The best odds of winning the game is to have balance, good hitting and good pitching, offense, and defense. Unfortunately, Wall Street has overlooked how important defense is to individual investors. They care deeply (Kahneman would argue twice as much) about playing defense and preventing major bear markets as much as they do about achieving good appreciation. This chapter is just another example of specific tools you can add to your tool chest to help you accomplish this.

Trend Strategy Number 2: Relative Strength

"Relative strength is a measure of the price trend of a stock or other financial instrument compared to another stock, instrument, or industry. It is calculated by taking the price of one asset and dividing it by another." (Source: Investopedia)

In other words, out of a handful of investments, whichever one has performed the best over a specified time frame has the highest relative strength. Hence, if one investment has a high relative strength, the conclusion we can arrive at is that its price has been trending up (compared to the other options).

The Dynamic Duo: A Basic (Yet Convincing) Example

What if we were to use relative strength to indicate whether we should own one of two traditional asset classes (stocks or bonds)? Using the SPDR S&P 500 ETF (SPY) to represent stocks and the iShares Core Total US Bond Market ETF (AGG) to represent bonds, we allocate 100 percent of our portfolio to whichever possesses the highest relative strength over the past six months. Is it possible this simple formula could lead to outperformance over time? Is it possible that this proactive strategy could also reduce risk?

Note: The idea of using a six month relative strength measurement is derived from the research and analysis found in James P. O'Shaughnessy's book *What Works on Wall Street*.

Relative Strength Filter: At the beginning of each month we select the ETF (representing a specific asset class) with the best six-month relative strength. We then allocate 100 percent of the portfolio to that one investment.

Using ETFReplay.com as our analysis tool, we can backtest to see how this relative strength strategy would have performed in both bull and bear markets, going back as far as 2004 when both ETFs were available for purchase.

The following graph shows the performance of this "Dynamic Duo" strategy (darker line) in comparison to the S&P 500 Index (lighter line).

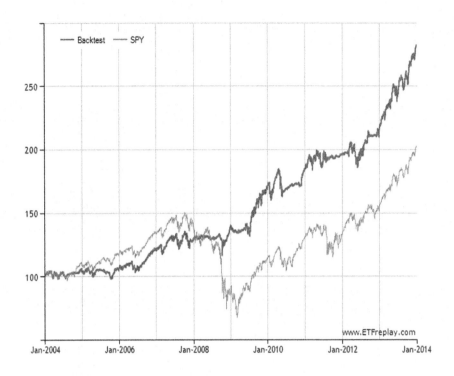

Stats

	Dynamic Duo	**SPY**
Total Return:	182.7%	103%
Annual Growth Rate:	11%	7.3%
Volatility:	11.7	20.4
Max Drawdown:	14.1%	55.2%
2004:	5.7%	10.7%
2005:	-1.1%%	4.8%
2006:	15.8%	15.8%
2007:	6.3%	5.1%
2008:	7.9%	-36.8%
2009:	21.4%	26.4%

2010:	8.6%	15.1%
2011:	7.4%	1.9%
2012:	8.6%	16%
2013:	32.3%	32.3%

Observations

- Notice that the Dynamic Duo *underperformed* the market in *five out of the ten years*, yet dramatically outpaced in total performance over that time frame. Again, what is your goal? Is it to outperform the market every year or beat a benchmark? I would prefer to have a strategy that will allow me to better preserve capital in major bear markets and still achieve reasonable growth in bull markets. **I am happy to lose some innings, as long as I know I can win the game.**
- The maximum drawdown for the Dynamic Duo is approximately one-quarter that of the S&P 500 buy-and-hold strategy, with almost half of the volatility.
- Only one down year (barely).
- The Dynamic Duo strategy will require approximately 1.5 changes of investment per year.

But the efficient market hypothesis says that the only way to outpace the all-knowing, all-inclusive market is to take on more risk. It makes you question conventional wisdom, doesn't it?

The Starting Five Portfolio: Putting it all Together, a Comprehensive Approach

What if we were to add a few more investment options to our relative strength analysis?

The next tactical/trend strategy encompasses numerous themes promoted within this book:

1. The use of exchange traded funds (ETFs).
2. The use of alternative asset classes (beyond just stocks, bonds, and cash).
3. The use of trend analysis via relative strength.
4. The use of nonemotional data-driven indicators to proactively adjust your portfolio (being tactical) and thereby adjusting with the current environment.
5. Playing both offense and defense.

If we were to select a short/manageable list of ETFs that can provide us exposure to different asset classes, what might that resemble? Just like the starting five on a basketball team, each player is unique and has a specific role to play. Here is our starting five:

1. Since the correlation matrix proved that most stocks move in synch, we just need one ETF to represent US stocks: **SPY** (SPDR S&P 500 Index).
2. We need some international stock exposure that isn't as highly correlated to the US market. Therefore, we will include some emerging market exposure: **EEM** (iShares MSCI Emerging Markets).
3. We need to include an alternative asset class: **GLD** (SPDR Gold Shares); gold can be a potential quality inflation hedge and has low correlation with stocks.
4. We need some bond exposure: **TLT** (iShares 20+ Year Treasury Bond), a potential quality deflation hedge.
5. Lastly, we need a cash substitute: **SHY** (iShares 1–3 Year Treasury Bond)

Relative Strength Filter: At the beginning of each month we select the ETF (representing a specific asset class) with the best six-month relative strength. We then allocate 100 percent of the portfolio to that one investment.

Using ETFReplay.com as our analysis tool we can backtest to see how this relative strength strategy would have performed in both bull and bear markets, going back as far as 2005 when all five ETFs were available for purchase.

The following graph shows the performance of the "Starting Five Strategy" (darker line) in comparison to the S&P 500 Index (lighter line).

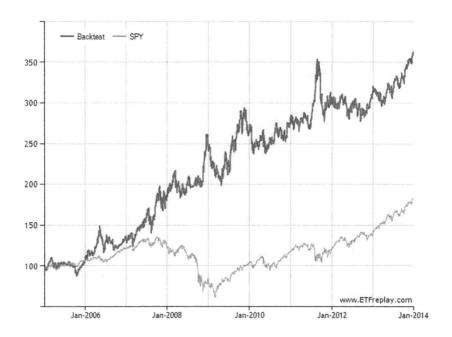

Stats

	The Starting Five	SPY
Total Return:	262.5%	83.4%
Annual Growth Rate:	15.4%	7.0%
Volatility:	22.2	21.1
Max Drawdown:	24%	55.2%
2005:	3.8%	4.8%
2006:	30.3%	15.8%
2007:	33.3%	5.1%
2008:	42%	-36.8%
2009:	2.6%	26.4%
2010:	7.1%	15.1%
2011:	9.3%	1.9%
2012:	2.1%	16%
2013:	15.5%	32.3%

Observations

- Notice that our Starting Five portfolio *underperformed* the market in *five out of the nine years*, yet dramatically outpaced in total performance over that time frame. Again, what is your goal? Is it to outperform the market every year or beat a benchmark? I would prefer to have a strategy that will allow me to better preserve capital in major bear markets and still achieve reasonable growth in bull markets. **I am happy to lose some of the battles, as long as I know I can win the war.**
- The maximum drawdown for our Starting Five portfolio is approximately half that of the S&P 500, yet overall volatility was a bit higher.
- No down years!
- The Starting Five strategy will require approximately three changes of investment per year.

7Twelve Relative Strength Portfolio: Applying Relative Strength to a Truly Diversified Portfolio

What if we were to add even more investment options to our relative strength analysis?

The next tactical/trend strategy applies tactical trend analysis to the diversified 7Twelve Portfolio. Keep in mind that the actual ETFs used in this analysis are not as important as the representation of the asset classes themselves.

The select list of ETFs used to represent the 7Twelve Portfolio:

1. Large Cap Stock: **SPY** (SPDR S&P 500 Index)
2. Mid Cap Stock: **IJH** (iShares Core S&P MidCap 400 Index)
3. Small Cap Stock: **VBR** (Vanguard U.S. SmallCap Value)
4. International Stock: **EFA** (iShares MSCI EAFE)
5. Emerging Markets: **VWO** (Vanguard FTSE Emerging Markets)
6. Real Estate: **VNQ** (Vanguard MSCI U.S. REIT)
7. Natural Resources: **IGE** (iShares S&P North American Natural Resources)
8. Commodities: **DBC** (PowerShares DB Commodity Index)
9. US Bonds: **AGG** (iShares Core Total US Bond)
10. Inflation Protected Bonds: **TIP** (iShares Barclays TIPS)
11. International Bonds: **BWX** (SPDR Barclays International Treasury Bond)
12. Cash: **SHY** (Barclays Low Duration Treasury)

Relative Strength Filter: At the beginning of each month we select the ETF (representing a specific asset class) with the best six-month relative strength. We then allocate 100 percent of the portfolio to that one investment.

Using ETFReplay.com as our analysis tool we can backtest to see how this relative strength strategy would have performed in both bull and bear markets, going back as far as 2006 when eleven of the twelve strategies were available for purchase. The International Bond ETF was created in 2007 and therefore was factored into the results one year into the analysis.

The following graph shows the performance of the 7Twelve Relative Strength Portfolio (darker line) in comparison to the S&P 500 Index (lighter line).

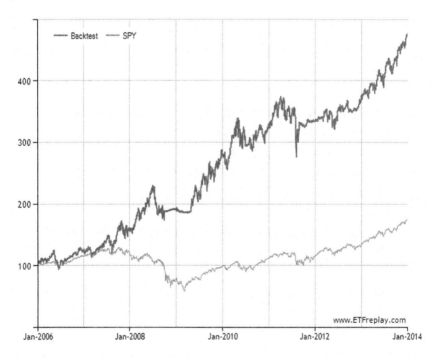

Stats

	7Twelve Relative Strength	**SPY**
Total Return:	377.1%	75%
Annual Growth Rate:	21.6%	7.3%
Volatility:	23.8	22.1
Max Drawdown:	26.2%	55.2%
2006:	25.4%	15.8%
2007:	24.6%	5.1%
2008:	22.8%	-36.8%
2009:	45.4%	26.4%
2010:	17.8%	15.1%
2011:	1.8%	1.9%
2012:	10.7%	16%
2013:	28.8%	32.3%

Observations

- The combination of trend analysis with true diversification can yield some impressive results.
- The maximum drawdown for our 7Twelve Relative Strength portfolio is approximately half that of the S&P 500, yet overall volatility was a bit higher.
- No down years!
- The 7Twelve Relative Strength Portfolio will require approximately four changes of investment per year.

In sum what we are accomplishing:

- We are not like most mutual funds that are handcuffed in our investment choice.
- We can change asset classes and even go to cash if the strategy warrants it.

- We are diversified in our options, but aren't required to hold a poor performer for extended periods of time (momentum reduces the odds of that occurring).
- We have hedges for many markets, including both inflationary and deflationary.
- We aren't guessing or going off of hunches or someone's hot tip or opinion; it is a data-driven (unemotional) system.
- No day trading is required. Changes only need to be analyzed and made once per month.
- Lastly, you are required to be more proactive and take on increased responsibility.

How do such systems mediate the behavioral tendencies analyzed in chapter two?

Loss Aversion: With dramatically less drawdown, these proactive strategies more efficiently address this behavioral characteristic. Conclusion: better than buy-and-hold.

Volatility: Volatility measures were half for the Dynamic Duo, but roughly equivalent for the Starting Five and 7Twelve Relative Strength portfolios. But again, in both cases largest drawdown statistics were dramatically reduced. Conclusion: better than buy-and-hold.

Anchoring: With less drawdown, less of an issue of anchoring. Conclusion: better than buy-and-hold.

Action Bias: The craving for constant analysis and action is fulfilled. Conclusion: better than buy-and-hold.

Herding: By implementing an unemotional, data-driven tactical strategy, there will be less directionless investing and susceptibility to outside input and influences (to follow the herd). Conclusion: better than buy-and-hold.

These portfolios are not meant to be the be-all and end-all. Rather, they are meant to represent how a basic, diversified, tactical trend portfolio can produce (and behave) in a manner unlike anything you may have become accustomed to.

As you can see by now, this is anything *but* buy-and-hold!

Interesting Observation: Relative strength strategies exhibit a lot of promise as indicated by James O'Shaughnessy's analysis in *What Works on Wall Street* in addition to the examples provided in this chapter. However, it is worth observing that relative strength success seems to be inconsistent with the failures of chasing returns exhibited by Israelsen's analysis found in chapter eight. My hypothesis is that trends in the financial markets tend to run their course over specific lengths of time, usually best measured in months not years. Perhaps a good analogy can be drawn when predicting the weather, or more specifically, rain storms. If it has been raining for an hour (time measurement) in Massachusetts there is a good chance that the rain will continue for another hour. However, to predict it will be raining tomorrow, one day later (time measurement), exhibits little to no correlation or predictive powers.

Other Fascinating Trends

In addition to price trends moving as a result of momentum, some additional trend-related phenomena are worth further investigation. At the very least they are worth a mention because they are just plain intriguing. I will not explain these other theories in great detail. However, I want to briefly mention these theories because I think they further validate the larger trend concept, that repeating patterns do occur over time.

- Dow Theory
- Presidential Cycle
- Seasonality

1) **Dow Theory:** Charles Dow created the Dow Theory at the turn of the twentieth century. The premise was simple. If goods were being produced and moving through the economy, then this would be reflected in the action of both the industrials and the transports (stock indexes). Both of them represent the makers and the transporters of the raw and finished products.

Those that follow this theory attempt to identify when trends change from bull to bear or from bear to bull. A new bull market is signaled when a decline in the markets *fails* to produce a *new* low in one or both of the indexes. A rally then follows, taking out the high of the previous rally. Conversely, a new bear market is signaled when a rise in the markets *fails* to produce a *new* high in one or both of the indexes. A decline then follows, taking out the low of the previous decline.

Does it work? Martin Pring, author of *Technical Analysis Explained*, using a version of the Dow Theory from the 1966 stock market top to just after the turn of the century, averaged about 13 percent per year. This is a few percentage points better than the market as a whole. As with our previously discussed trend strategies, the major advantage of this theory is that it helps the investor sidestep the steep market drawdowns.

Definitions can sometimes be cumbersome to digest. Therefore, to make your life easier, you might want to simply reference a website that provides you with the current Dow Theory signal. Such a website can be found here: http://dowtheorybook.com/.

2) **Presidential Cycle:** In Jeffrey Hirsch's book *The Little Book of Stock Market Cycles*, he notes that wars and recessions tend to happen within the first two years of most four-year

presidential terms, while prosperity and bull markets tend to be found in the final two years of the cycle. According to this theory, the government carries out the least popular policies when job security is at its highest. As elections draw near, the government is motivated to implement policies that are more popular, and thus bull markets take hold.

Does it work? Hirsch points out that in forty-four presidential administrations since 1833, the last two years of four-year presidencies produced a total net market gain of 724 percent. Meanwhile, the first two years only produced 273.1 percent total net market gains. The return numbers are evidence that government influence affects the trends of the markets.

3) **Seasonal Patterns:** Have you ever heard the saying "Sell in May and go away"? This saying is tied to the seasonal patterns of market returns. Each year marks a new beginning and renewed optimism, along with the recent sales numbers from the holiday season, tends to start off strong. Eventually spring leads to summer, and the nice weather signals the peak vacation time, especially for Wall Street, and buying slows down. Eventually autumn arrives, kids go back to school, and it is time to play catch-up from the light summer months. After September, the historically worst month of the year, is behind everyone, money managers focus on ending the year with strong numbers and opportunities for bonuses, which once again beefs up the market. Historically, the months between November 1 and April 30 of the subsequent year are by far the best months to have exposure to the stock market.

Does it work? Hirsch notes that $10,000 invested in 1950 in the Dow Jones Industrial Average and invested only during the best six months (November through April) of the year would have grown to $674,073 by 2012. Meanwhile, if that same $10,000 were invested during the historically worst six months (May through October) of the year, it would have resulted in a loss of -$1,024. Again, these results are undeniable. It appears that our annual societal behavior patterns have led to an undeniable trend.

As the cliché investment disclosure goes: past results are no guarantee for future results. However, these studies should provide for a high level of confidence that it has worked for a long time and that markets do move in trends.

So why does trend-following work? Why aren't more investment companies recommending these types of strategies? I believe most fund companies don't want you moving money in and out of a manger's hands on a regular basis. Therefore, they discourage such actions. This is one of the reasons that a lot of mutual funds have a short-term trading fee—these don't exist with ETFs—that they will impose if you haven't held the investment for an extended period of time. I believe the industry also views this as risky. Undisciplined and uneducated investors will do more harm to themselves than good by trading on emotions rather than a disciplined strategy. The key, again, is using unemotional, disciplined triggers. That is what trend-analysis is all about.

This is a good transition into the negatives and drawbacks of this strategy. They are very real and need to be considered.

1. Trend-following requires steadfast discipline. To follow such a strategy, you will need to check your signals consistently. Everyone's life is busy with vacations, weddings, illness, etc., but the market is indifferent to you. If it is open, you will need to monitor it.

2. Trend-following, as outlined above, follows longer-term trends and signals only after—sometimes a long while after—a top or bottom is reached. You will have to come to grips with the fact that you will never sell at the absolute top or buy at the absolute bottom. Moreover, it cannot prevent or protect you from a dramatically quick decline, such as the stock market crash of 1987. Then again, neither will buy-and-hold.
3. Trend-following may underperform in a strong bull market.
4. There will be times when you suffer multiple losing trades in a row. For moving averages, painful whipsaws can occur when the market dances with volatility above and below your moving average indicator. This forces you to purchase at miniature peaks and to suffer multiple small losses. This is bound to happen, and there is no way to avoid it. However, if you remain committed to your strategy, these whipsaws eventually end and longer-term trends always develop. For relative strength there may be consecutive months when the investment that exhibited the most relative strength pulls back. Experiencing these actions is perhaps the most difficult aspect of trend-following, and it is something that you must mentally resign yourself to before you implement it.

In summary, this strategy is beneficial because:

- The system is unemotional.
- It is easy to research.
- It has worked in the past.
- It empowers the individual investor and eliminates helplessness.
- It can provide protection from bear markets (similar to 2008).

- It allows investors to play both offense and defense (balanced tactical game plan).

Another positive caveat of this strategy is that it is easy to analyze trigger points. All you have to do is to visit an online finance page (e.g., Yahoo finance, Google finance, CNBC, MarketWatch, etc.). Then you click on a chart of the S&P 500 and add a technical indicator. Choose a moving average of your choice, and in less than a minute you have your moving average indicator line on your chart. In fact, you can even save that page as a favorite, and it will update for you on a daily basis.

For relative strength readings you can follow your portfolios in Morningstar or reference websites like VectorGrader that regularly update performance of various ETF asset classes (www.vectorgrader.com/strats/market-rotation).

ETFs are the perfect investment tool to use when implementing the strategies outlined in this chapter. With ETFs, you will not incur the short-term trading fees that many mutual fund companies issue. You determine the percentage of your portfolio that you would like to allocate to this type of strategy. How much you earmark to these strategies all depends on what you feel comfortable with and think you can proactively manage.

We are in extreme monetary policy times, and bubbles seem to be occurring on a more regular basis. Considering Jack Bogle's comments of anticipated market corrections (see chapter one), what should be your course of action? Should you use trend analysis for 100 percent of your stock exposure, just a small portion, or should you just stick with buy-and-hold?

There is no one solution. However, for those hesitant to fully embrace tactical strategies, I like Paul Merriman's comments in his May 1, 2013, article on the MarketWatch website "Nine Steps to Surviving a Financial Apocalypse." He said, "I hold half of my portfolio on a buy-and-hold basis, using index funds, and the other half using mechanical market timing, which is not dependent on forecasts, opinions, or judgments. These two approaches are not correlated, and the combination gives me peace of mind."

Don't underestimate the value of a peace of mind strategy!

He continues, "In good times, my buy-and-hold portfolio almost always does better. During bad times, my timed portfolio almost always does better. There's always part of my portfolio that makes me feel that I am participating in what's working well, and there's always another part that gives me a sense of protection."

You can read the article here: http://www.marketwatch.com/story/9-steps-to-surviving-the-financial-apocalypse-2013-05-01.

The most important message to gain from this chapter is that you do not have to be helpless when major bear markets hit. Severe bear markets like the one in 2008 can create a lot of stress and anxiety, especially for those who are close to or in retirement. This chapter presented proactive strategies that can help you play defense against such declines. Believe it or not, you can actually win by not losing.

Additional Resources:

- CXO Advisory Group, LLC provides in-depth analytical research into markets and momentum strategies: http://www.cxoadvisory.com/
- Dark Liquidity tracks the performance of various trend-following strategies: http://dark-liquidity.com/homepage.php.
- ETFReplay provides comprehensive backtesting for ETF strategies: http://www.etfreplay.com/

- Keller Partners' blog provides weekly updates on the direction of the markets: http://www.kellerpartners.com/category/blog/
- Meb Faber's blog provides regular insights in market data and technical analysis research: http://mebfaber.com/
- Michael Covel's books, blog, and podcasts are all about trend trading: http://www.michaelcovel.com.
- VectorGrader's website tracks a lot of stock market technical indicators as well as fundamental valuations. http://www.vectorgrader.com/.
- Wishing Wealth Blog provides daily updates on the direction of the markets: http://wishingwealthblog.com/

> **In Summary**
> - Avoiding the major market downdrafts is equally important, if not more important, than realizing the major market up moves.
> - You can win by not losing.
> - The markets tend to move in trends over time.
> - *Disciplined* tactical management can help you implement these philosophies in an unemotional way.

We find that trend-following has delivered strong positive returns and realized a low correlation to traditional asset classes each decade for more than a century.

—AQR Capital Management: *A Century of Evidence on Trend-Following Investing*

CHAPTER 10

SELF-DIRECTED RETIREMENT ACCOUNTS

Question: Have you ever wished you could invest in real tangible assets, such as rental properties, within your IRA?

Since you have gotten this far through the book, I hope that you have learned some bold ideas and concepts.

While the previous suggestions were outside of the box of conventional Wall Street, this next topic obliterates that box completely.

The following is an outline of an investment strategy—more like an investment philosophy—that very few people are aware of and even fewer have implemented. In 2011, I met Michael Hajek III, CPA. Until then, I had only a cursory familiarity with this tactic, and I had never seen anyone successfully implement it. As of the publishing of this book, I have not yet implemented this strategy in my own planning. This has been due to certain affiliations and constrictions between brokers and dealers. Having said that, I feel that this information not only complements our previous discussions, but it would also be a disservice to omit it.

The concept of the self-directed IRA (abbreviated here as SDI) is alternative investing on steroids. It is the same approach that many of the wealthiest investors in the country, such as Mitt Romney, implement (http://learningcenter.theentrustgroup.com/pages/course/portal.aspx?courseid=309). As with most advanced investment strategies, this one also requires a greater level of due diligence and responsibility on the part of the investor. Whether you consider this strategy for implementation or you just read about this to expand your spectrum of investment possibilities, I think that you will find this information as fascinating as I did.

As my understanding and knowledge of this topic is not firsthand, I felt it best to hear directly from someone who, as a CPA, has educated others and personally implemented this strategy. Therefore, I have asked Mr. Hajek to contribute directly to this section by sharing with you his insights on a strategy that is increasingly gaining traction as investors seek proactive, tax-efficient, and creative means of creating wealth.

An Introduction to Self-Directed IRAs:

I would first like to take this opportunity to thank Tim for including me in his project and for allowing me the occasion to share with his readers such a fascinating topic.

By way of introduction, when I started my CPA practice in 1995, the universe of alternative investing was even less an option than it is today. Often, clients were looking for investment vehicles that afforded not only a rate of return and tax efficiency but also the ability to have more control over how and where assets set aside for retirement were invested.

According to the August 9, 2009, publishing of "**Retirement Savings and Household Wealth in 2007**," the **Congressional Research Service** reported that "In 2007, 53 percent of US households owned at least one retirement account, whether an individual retirement account, a 401(k) plan, or other employment-based retirement account. The median combined balance of all retirement accounts owned by households with at least one account was $45,000. Twenty-five percent of households had total retirement account balances of $140,000 or more."

In addition, research shows that "total US retirement assets hit a new record high of $19.5 trillion as of December 31, 2012" and "retirement savings accounted for 36 percent of all household financial assets in the United States at the end of 2012." http://www.ici.org/pdf/2013_factbook.pdf.

With an increasing number of dollars being saved for retirement by US families, investors are often faced with the increasing challenge of finding opportunities for their assets. For most, the answer has been to turn to Wall Street as they have been convinced that the stock market is the only option available.

"Because the majority of assets held in retirement accounts are invested in stocks, trends in stock prices have a significant impact on households' retirement account balances." (Congressional Research Service: "Retirement Savings and Household Wealth in 2007")

In the following pages, we intend to relay several concepts. First, Wall Street is not your only option for your pretax investments. Additionally, by using retirement funds to make the same investment you could make with after-tax money, you not only improve the tax efficiency of your investment but could also concurrently improve the diversification of your total portfolio.

Though hidden from mainstream discussions, there are alternatives to Wall Street for your retirement dollars. Finding investments not tied to traditional financial products is not a new concept; in fact, alternative investing is a well-known successful strategy utilized by large endowments. Traditionally having produced higher than average returns than the common investor, endowments often place a portion of their investment portfolios in Wall Street but also divert a segment into alternative opportunities. http://www.investopedia.com/articles/financial-theory/09/ivy-league-endowments-money-management.asp

Endowments have a few advantages over the common investor, which are important factors influencing their success:

1. Dollars – endowments deal with sums of money that are multiples of what the common investor has available, thereby affording them the option of building their own nonmarket opportunities.
2. Taxation – endowments have the benefit of being exempt from paying taxes.
3. Time Horizon – not constrained by the same liquidity requirements, endowments have a considerably longer time horizon.

While the common investor cannot compete with large endowments in size and scope, it is possible to adopt a similar strategy of utilizing alternative investment opportunities in addition to traditional financial products. As they are reserved for retirement, pretax dollars typically have the longest time horizon and are tax efficient as gains/losses are deferred (or tax free in the case of Roth IRA funds) until their withdrawal. By "self-directing" retirement dollars, the common investor can potentially emulate the success of the large endowments by implementing long-term, tax-efficient alternative investments.

The term "self-directed" essentially means that investors maintain control over where their qualified (retirement) funds are invested. In most households, retirement accounts hold traditional Wall Street-packaged products, such as stocks, bonds, mutual funds, etc. While the self-directed accounts can hold these products as well, they also have the ability to hold other potentially appreciating assets, some of the most common being real estate, mortgages, private loans and notes, and tax liens. While it is a vast topic, and there are some constraints, there are vast opportunities available.

Most sophisticated investors have at least a basic understanding of the value of rental real estate. As an excellent introduction to the SDI, let's look into the differences between using IRA dollars and personal cash to make a purchase.

Let's assume for a moment the following criteria:

Jack is an airline pilot; he has $200,000 in the bank and $200,000 in his IRA. His tax bracket is 30 percent. In his neighborhood, a house that is move-in ready just went on the market for $150,000, and he would like to purchase and rent it for $2,000 per month.

> **Option One: Using the Cash**
>
> Jack can make the purchase by depleting his cash in the bank and have rental income added to his personal tax return. After taxes, his annual rate of return on the property would be 11.2 percent ($2,000 x 12)-30 percent/$150,000.

> **Option Two: Using the IRA**
>
> Jack makes the same purchase using the value of his IRA by self-directing. Because the rental income is paid back to the IRA and he does not do so personally, the income is tax deferred, realizing an annual rate of return of 16 percent ($2,000 x 12)/$150,000.

Of course, this is an oversimplified example, but the fundamentals remain consistent. The SDI is a strategy that utilizes pretax dollars outside of the Wall Street model, giving the owner direct control over the asset in addition to the rate of return.

"Sell the sizzle, not the steak"

Americans love meat, and a great steak tops the list of many people's choice of entrée. For consumers, there are many options for purchasing a good steak, whether you are dining in a five-star restaurant, picking it up from the local butcher, or even going down to the farm. The difference lies in the amount of effort the consumer is willing to commit to the meal.

When dining at a five-star restaurant, consumers expect to pay a premium because they are buying more than just the steak. Preparation, presentation, and ambiance are all costs that are built into the menu price. Paying more is accepted because the consumer relinquishes the responsibility of the meal experience.

At the local butcher, the additional costs of preparation, presentation, and ambiance are removed from the cost of the steak, thus making it less expensive. The work falls to the consumer to prepare and serve, as the steak is uncooked and wrapped in paper rather than ready to eat and served on a china plate.

In the case of the five-star restaurant or the butcher shop, there are still additional overhead costs. Transportation, staffing, and storage are always factors. By driving to the farm and picking your own cow, you can avoid these costs, reducing the price per ounce even further. The tradeoff is that the consumer will have even more work to do.

To further our discussion on the benefits of the SDI, let's use the American love affair with a great steak as a metaphor. In this scenario, Wall Street is our five-star restaurant. The consumer (i.e., the investor) pays a premium for the investment, the packaging, and the ambiance. When you visit with many financial planning firms, the advisors will show you a menu of ready-to-order investment choices. The investor will choose and pay for the product. The prepackaged, plated result is delivered the way that Wall Street wants to serve it with minimal effort on the part of the consumer.

With the advent of self-trading platforms, a consumer can buy and sell from the same Wall Street menu, but there is no ambiance. There is no advisor showing you a set of choices based on his or her perceptions of time horizon, risk tolerance, and goals. The consumers do their own research, analysis, and product purchases. They reduce the costs, but they take on much more of the responsibility. Instead of having an hour-long meeting with your planner to review your investment options, you spend hours examining PE ratios and standard deviations on the computer and/or taking notes from stock market talk shows. This is the equivalent of patronizing your local butcher, picking your steak, and examining the cut, age, and size. You choose how the steak is prepared, cooked, and served.

It should be obvious that utilizing the SDI strategy is comparable to driving out to a country farm and choosing not just the steak but also the cow it comes from. This scenario requires dramatically more work and responsibility, as you are the one who researches and selects the farm and the cow. Moreover, you provide the transport, the storage, and are in charge of the preparation. Following this analogy, as an SDI investor, you are no longer constrained by the options available on a predetermined menu or on a preset inventory of selections.

The point is that any of these options will get you a steak. If you are the type of investor who prefers a prepackaged, plated selection, then the traditional Wall Street menu is available. However, if you are willing to put more personal effort into taking control of your investment dollars, then let's continue to explore the world of the SDI.

It is not accidental that we began our introduction into SDIs with the example of rental real estate. Investors have long thought of real estate as an alternative investment to the stock market and the Wall Street way of building assets. As a result, it is also one of the most common purchases using self-directed assets.

Of course, Wall Street recognizes the benefits of owning real estate as well. With the introduction of ETFs and other investment vehicles, Wall Street has found a way to redraw the box around what was once an alternative to the stock market, making it marketable, compensatable, and under their control, thereby adding it to their prepackaged menu of investment choices.

Another option that Wall Street has designed for investors interested in owning real estate is the development of the REIT (Real Estate Investment Trust). As REITs were discussed in detail in earlier chapters, we will not reintroduce the concept except to say that purchasers are afforded the opportunity to have partial ownership of real estate that they may not otherwise have the means to own, and the operational/managerial concerns of things like collecting rent, negotiating leases, and maintaining the property fall to the REIT and not the investor.

As a part of the Wall Street menu, the purchase of real estate comes with all the staples of in-the-box investing. There are prospectuses, performance reports, agreements and contribution requirements, private placement memorandums, glossy presentation folders, commissions, and fees. All of this is packaged and delivered right to the table, ready to consume.

Utilizing the SDI is a way for investors to take back the alternative investing that Wall Street has packaged for them.

Building your own REIT

Jack, our airline pilot, has done exactly that. Rather than investing all of his retirement funds into Wall Street, he saw an opportunity to make the same purchase he intended to make with his after-tax cash, but he utilized his tax-deferred dollars instead. He thereby diversified his IRA portfolio (150K Real Estate/50K Traditional Investing), and maximized the rate of return on the rental (16 percent versus 11 percent). As an added bonus, Jack did not have to drain his personal cash for the investment. By utilizing his long-term retirement dollars, his personal cash is free for other needs or wants.

Renting the property is not Jack's only option. Reselling and realizing a gain or loss in his SDI account (the results of which are also tax deferred) is at his discretion. This is often an overlooked advantage of the SDI; time and again real estate investors will not liquidate during market peaks out of fear or distaste of the tax effect. Through tax-deferred purchases, buying and selling are truly driven by the market; opportunities for profit from an investment are not curtailed by concerns over taxation.

Depending on your perspective, there are some advantages that the Wall Street model has over the SDI. For the purposes of diversification, Wall Street products typically invest in multiple real estate opportunities; Jack's one rental house could be damaged in a flood or some other disaster, making it impossible for him to rent or sell it. Spreading that risk over multiple properties does limit exposure.

In addition, the Wall Street model comes with the assumption that the investment has been vetted, researched, and reviewed by individuals that deem it recommendable, suitable, and sellable. For self-directed investors, this due diligence falls on them alone. Is the real estate in a good neighborhood? How much repair and maintenance will it need? Should the value increase in the holding time frame? The SDI is no panacea; while offering additional opportunity, it brings with it an increased responsibility, potential risk, and possibility for error.

Real estate is far from the only investment option available in the SDI. As we mentioned, the investing opportunities are vast. The following are some unique investments that have been implemented using the self-directed model to potentially generate returns.

Fishing Rights

Mr. Smith, the owner of a construction company and avid fisherman, was approached by a business associate with an investment opportunity. The associate was a prominent restaurateur, who was well known for personally catching and serving fish each day. Through his experience with other local fishermen, the restaurateur discovered an opportunity, few new existed. Seeking capital, the restaurateur approached Mr. Smith for a loan in order to broker fishing rights.

A fishing right is a way in which the government can provide oversight on the amount of fish that commercial fishermen remove from our oceans. A right includes a quota on the amount of fish that can be caught each day. Fishermen must purchase rights for the amount of fish they catch, and the rights expire within a specified time period. For the sake of this explanation, let's assume one right is equivalent to one pound of fish. A fisherman purchases five hundred rights, and therefore he is able to catch no more than five hundred pounds of fish on that day. If he catches less than five hundred pounds, the rights expire and he has spent money that he did not need to. This eats into the profits of fish that he did catch. For this reason, most fishermen do not purchase more rights than the amount of fish they think they will catch.

As fishing is unpredictable, there are occurrences where more fish are caught than rights purchased. Herein lies the investment opportunity. The restaurateur purchases fishing rights on a daily basis; as the boats come in for the day, if they have caught more fish than they have rights, the fishermen would require additional rights to bring in the additional haul, rights available and sold at a premium by the restaurateur.

Mr. Smith's investment was in the form of a loan to the restaurateur. Mr. Smith secured this loan by a stock pledge of the restaurant and a personal guarantee from the borrower that he or she would pay back the loan in monthly installments at a specified interest rate. Therefore, the investment itself is not dependent on whether or not fish rights are actually sold.

The loan was made directly from Mr. Smith's Roth IRA (a nondeductible IRA that grows tax deferred and at retirement can be withdrawn tax free, additional details in next chapter). Loan payments are made monthly directly to the Roth IRA. The restaurateur has the funds to buy and sell fish rights; Mr. Smith maintains control over his retirement funds and increases the value by the specified interest rate on the loan.

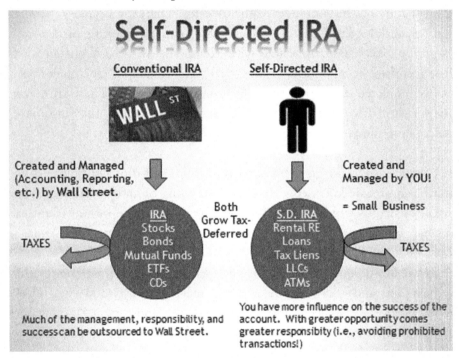

Invest in What You Know!

One of the fundamental keys of any successful investment, whether it is in the traditional market or whether you are self-directing your assets, is knowledge. Although each investor should perform his or her own due diligence with traditional market investing, most take advantage of the resources provided by a financial advisor and review provided educational materials and legal prospectuses for key information on the terms and risks involved prior to placing money.

While it is imperative that you seek out the advice of a professional (e.g., a CPA, an attorney, or a real estate agent) when self-directing your investments, the vetting of a good investment or a poor investment opportunity falls squarely on the shoulders of the investor. There are no glossy educational materials or prospectus; in fact, most financial planning professionals are unable to assist investors with SDI assets as it is in conflict with their securities licensing and broker–dealer relationship. Remember, these are not preplated steaks that someone brings to your table. These are cows. The investor drives to the farm, chooses the cow, the cut, the seasoning, the cooking temperature, etc.

So how do we choose good investments for our self-directed funds? How do we acquire the knowledge and understanding of an opportunity? The simple answer is experience. With self-directing, it is important to invest in what you know.

Everyone has unique knowledge or skills. Everyone has something that he or she understands very well. Maybe it's the real estate in your own neighborhood. Maybe it's knowledge about motorcycles or landscaping. Within your specific knowledge base, there are ample open doors for potential profits.

For example, a rancher who has no faith in his understanding of the stock market but has full knowledge of land prices would be able to utilize his knowledge for this type of investment. Land speculation would be considered risky by most, but the rancher has intimate knowledge of land growth. It isn't as risky for someone with specialized knowledge like him. Therefore, he can feel very comfortable purchasing tracts of land in his IRA. This provides the rancher a better feeling of control and safety, as opposed to allowing a hedge fund manager to purchase oil contracts or some other speculative investment.

Let's look at some additional "real-life" examples of people utilizing their specific knowledge to seek out investment opportunities for their qualified accounts.

A Storm of Opportunity

Amy is an avid diver who used to frequently travel to the Cayman Islands for both recreation and business. As part of her travels, she would often research and price real estate opportunities in the area.

Over several years of visits, she was amazed at the rate of appreciation in island real estate, and she became discouraged when property costs remained outside of her budget. In September 2004, Hurricane Ivan devastated the Cayman Islands. As a result, real estate prices drastically fell and remained depressed while the island recuperated. Utilizing her IRA, Amy was able to negotiate a cash purchase of a piece of real estate, while other investors scrambled to find financing.

With her ownership secured, Amy began informing fellow divers and clubs of the availability of the property. Within a year, the property was 100 percent rented during the peak season. The island had recovered from the storm and the property values were restored to prestorm prices. The value of Amy's IRA not only increased by the rental income, but it also increased with the value of the real estate. This was a truly tax-efficient strategy.

Becoming the Bank

When it comes to getting a return on an investment, the banking model is the Holy Grail. The banking industry has long held the foothold on financing products structured to make the highest return with the least amount of risk. In recent years, changes in the economy, along with increasing regulations and tightening internal procedures, has created a lending labyrinth. This has restricted the flow of money from most financial institutions to those with a need or desire to obtain financing and lines of credit. The result of restrained bank lending has created an opportunity for the individual investor to model the success of the banking industry by providing a less complicated access to capital. Many established and start-up businesses offer an opportunity for investors looking to diversify their portfolio. In addition, short- and long-term real estate loans, and smaller dollar loans which are often neglected by lending institutions, offer a potentially profitable opportunity.

Micro Machine

There are two things in his life that Joe valued above all else: his wife and his Harley. Each year, he, his wife, and some friends made the pilgrimage across central Florida to participate in Daytona Beach Bike Week. During one of his trips, a good friend he often rode with expressed an interest in purchasing a new motorcycle. However, due to some credit issues, he was becoming increasingly frustrated in his attempts to obtain financing through traditional lending institutions.

Having recently opened a self-directed account with a portion of his IRA funds, Joe had been looking for an opportunity just like this one. After agreeing to the terms, Joe contacted his attorney, who drafted the legal documents. Joe's qualified funds provided a loan to his friend of 80 percent on the motorcycle's value with an interest rate of 7.25 percent for five years and were secured by the motorcycle itself. The borrower made payments directly to the IRA account, and Joe's assets grew tax deferred.

In the case of a default on the loan, Joe could repossess the motorcycle and sell the asset based on market demand. By only providing 80 percent of the purchase, Joe has secured equity in the loan to account for decreases in value. In addition, the legal documents required proof of insurance on the motorcycle in case of partial or total damage.

Don't Wine About It

In recent years, investors have had an increasing interest in collectable wines. Larry, an avid wine connoisseur, noticed this trend. Watching prices increase as a result of the demand, Larry recognized an opportunity to invest in an appreciating commodity.

Collectibles like fine wine are one of the few things that are prohibited in self-directed accounts. However, by applying a special exception to defined benefit plans, Larry was able to self-direct 20 percent of his investable assets directly into wine. He allocated an additional 10 percent to wine futures, thereby tailoring his passion for wine and knowledge from his business experience into a tax-deferred opportunity while diversifying his assets away from the traditional market.

Common investments with the SDI

The traditional market is an important part of an investor's retirement portfolio. However, to truly diversify your assets, the SDI can be a unique and potentially profitable alternative to the stock market for those willing to put in the time and effort.

Although this is by no means an inclusive list, investment options for your SDI can include the following:

- Business Financing
- LLCs
- Micro Loans
- Tax Liens
- Mortgages & Notes
- Private Placements & Private Stock
- Precious Metals
- Structured Settlements

- Livestock
- Rights & Warrants
- Accounts Receivable Factoring
- Bridge Loans

In addition to the traditional and Roth IRAs, most qualified funds can in fact be self-directed, giving the investor the opportunity to diverge some of his or her investable assets away from the Wall Street model.

Some examples of the types of accounts that are self-directed include the following:

- SEP IRAs
- Simple IRAs
- Keogh Plans
- Defined Benefit Plans
- Defined Contribution Plans
- Deferred Compensation Plans
- Solo 401(k)s
- Health Savings Accounts

One noteworthy observation is that the account types that cannot utilize the SDI strategy are the same ones that limit many of the other strategies discussed earlier in the book. These include the most popular retirement savings vehicles, 403(b) plans and group 401(k)s (unless specific provisions are allowed for self-directing), and the 529 college savings plan, the most popular college savings vehicle.

Prohibited Transactions

As with any investment, the SDI has its own set of specific rules and regulations referred to as prohibited transactions. Violating these rules could bring with it stiff IRS penalties, including the forfeiture of the tax-deferred nature of your entire qualified account balance in one year. As with any investment, it is important to fully understand what is allowed and what is not.

Some of the most common mistakes include:

- **Disqualified Persons**: IRS regulations specifically state that disqualified persons include the IRA holder and his or her spouse, in addition to their lineal descendants (children and grandchildren) and lineal ascendants (parents and grandparents). In addition, disqualified persons include investment advisers, managers, and fiduciaries, or any corporation, partnership, trust, or estate in which any of the above owns 50 percent or more of an interest.

- **Comingling of Funds**: One of the most common mistakes of the SDI investor is mixing qualified and nonqualified funds. As an example, an investor uses his or her IRA to purchase rental real estate. With funds from his or her personal checking account, the IRA owner purchases a shower curtain from a hardware store for use in the property. By paying for the shower curtain with nonqualified funds in the property, the funds have been comingled, and the entire value of the account, including the real estate, could be deemed taxable under review.

- **Sweat Equity**: Sweat equity is when the IRA owner performs work on the asset. For example, the IRA owner might paint the interior of the rental property rather than hiring a painter. By not having the expense of the painter, the investor has profited from his or her action. Personally profiting from the IRA investment is a prohibited transaction.

- **Prohibited Holdings:** While the types of investments for the SDI are much broader than that of traditional Wall Street investing, the IRS has deemed a few items as unsuitable for self-directed accounts; these include collectibles and life insurance contracts.

> These are just a few of the most common mistakes.
> It is important to seek proper advice from professionals such as CPAs, attorneys, and custodians
> who are experienced with self-directed IRAs
> prior to making any investment.

A Special Note on UBIT

In some circumstances, an IRA's investment activity can result in a taxable effect in the current year. This is called UBIT (unrelated business income tax). Specifically, UBIT is levied when an IRA owns real estate with debt or financing, payments on personal property, or income on an operating business within the IRA, as well as other instances.

While UBIT concerns should not prevent investment, it is important to be aware of its presence. You should consult a tax professional prior to investing.

Summary

"As of year-end 2011, total assets in tax-qualified retirement systems in the United States totaled $18.0 trillion, an increase of 35.3% since 2004," http://www.ebri.org/publications/benfaq/index.cfm?fa=retfaq4 and for most that means investing those assets in the traditional investment vehicles of Wall Street.

However, by following the example of some of the most consistently successful investment models, common investors can take additional control over their assets and emulate the alternative methods implemented. The world of the self-directed IRA does not come without risks. As with any investment, it is the responsibility of the owner to seek out proper advice, acquire an understanding of the hazards, and be aware of the regulations and limitations before investing.

Know what you own, and know why you own it.

—Peter Lynch

CHAPTER 11

TAX-EFFICIENT INVESTING FOR YOUR RETIREMENT AND COLLEGE GOALS

In the last chapter, we outlined how entrepreneurial investors can be more tax efficient by utilizing the lesser-known self-directed IRA. However, tax efficiency is universally important to all investors. Therefore, this chapter will outline the most common tax-favored accounts for you to potentially implement one or many of the strategies discussed in this book.

Choosing the right investments is important, but choosing the right investments within the right tax-efficient account is just as valuable. One of the best ways to grow your money is by being tax conscious and by preventing taxes from creating a drag on returns.

Since the strategies discussed in this book are more tactical (more hands-on and less buy-and-hold), you can assume that they are also less tax efficient. Hence these strategies may be best suited for tax-deferred accounts, of which there are various types.

The three terms we need to know:

1. Tax Deductible
2. Tax Deferred
3. Tax Free

Tax Deductible

Tax deductible means that the dollars you place inside of a tax-deductible account will lower your current taxable income and thus save you money on taxes up front. For example, if you earn $100,000 and you invest $10,000 into your 401(k) (a tax-deductible account), you will only be taxed on $90,000 of income. For simplicity sake, let's assume that your effective tax rate is 25 percent. A tax-deductible investment of $10,000 might save you approximately $2,500 in taxes. Theoretically, if you were to invest the $2,500 in an account, you would be 25 percent ahead of another investor who did not take advantage of a tax deduction. Perhaps this investor just invested in a taxable brokerage account. Your ability to grow $12,500 instead of $10,000 will compound over time and provide a huge benefit.

For example, the numbers below show the growth of $10,000 versus $12,500 over fifteen years, assuming a 6 percent growth rate:

$10,000 at 6 percent for fifteen years = $24,541

$12,500 at 6 percent for fifteen years = $30,676

That is a $6,135 difference over fifteen years.

*Note: Tax-deductible accounts will be taxed upon removal.

Tax Deferred

Tax deferral implies that as the investment generates income in the form of dividends, interest, and capital gains, you will not have to claim that as income on your current year's taxes. For example, people who invest in certificates of deposits that are not in a tax-deferred account have to claim that interest each year and pay taxes on that income. As the CD kicks off that interest, it becomes taxable to the investor, which wouldn't be the case if that same CD were held within a tax-deferred account.

For example, the numbers below show what an investor with a 25 percent effective tax rate would have to earn within a taxable account to yield the equivalent in a tax-deferred account.

Tax-free/exempt yield = 6 percent

Percentage of income you pay in taxes = 25 percent

Taxable equivalent yield = 8 percent

In the above example, you would have to yield a full 2 percent more of taxable income to break even with nontaxable income.

Perhaps one of the most eye-opening statistics that can be viewed within the Morningstar system is the tax drag of income-producing investments. The popular Vanguard Total Bond Market Inv (VBMFX) mutual fund, for example, reports a pretax rate of return of 5.63 percent and a post-tax rate of 3.76 percent return (found on the tax tab within Morningstar). This is a noteworthy difference.

5.63 percent versus 3.76 percent

The next chart shows a hypothetical $10,000 investment, returning a steady 6 percent in three tax situations: tax deferred, a 20 percent rate (assuming 15 percent federal and 5 percent state tax rates), and a 40 percent (assuming 35 percent federal and 5 percent state tax rates rate). As you can see, the tax deferral allows accounts to grow unimpeded by taxes and accumulate much faster.

(Source: John Hancock, http://www.jhinvestments.com/Article.aspx?ArticleID=%7BEAD829D7-2052-4B0A-8B1E-6B21E5DCF3DA%7D)

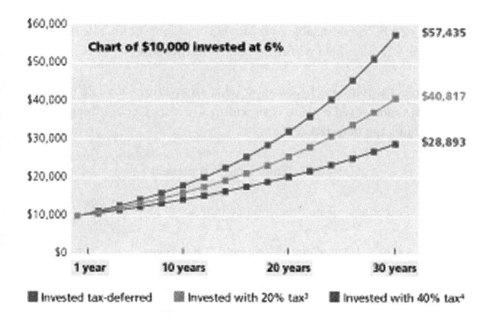

The more you can defer taxes, the faster your nest egg will grow.

In summary, you should not overlook the opportunity for tax deferral. This especially holds true for tactical management strategies that tend to trade frequently and produce a lot of capital gains.

The vehicles mentioned in this chapter that only offer tax deferral (no deductibility or tax-free withdrawals of growth) are tax-deferred variable annuities and nondeductible traditional IRAs.

Tax Free

One of the most tax-efficient ways to grow your money is within a tax-free account. There is no upfront tax deduction, but money will grow tax deferred. In addition, assuming you meet specific requirements, you can withdraw 100 percent of the account without paying any taxes. In other words, once you invest money into a tax-free account, you will never pay taxes on those dollars ever again, assuming all protocols are handled properly.

By combining the investment strategies outlined in this book, along with the right tax-advantaged account, you will maximize the effectiveness of your portfolio. To clarify which commonly utilized accounts fall within the tax-deductible, tax-deferred, and tax-free spectrum, I have provided some specific details about each type of account below.

The most common tax-deductible and tax-deferred accounts are 401(k)s, 403(b)s, traditional IRAs, accounts specific for business owners, SEP IRAs, simple IRAs, solo 401(k)s, and defined benefit plans.

The most common tax-deferred and tax-free accounts are Roth IRAs, Roth 401(k)s, 529 college savings plans, and Coverdell education savings accounts.

Note: Below I will focus on contribution limits, income restrictions, and investment control. For more specifics about these account options, further research on your part is recommended. All information below is based on 2014 tax guidelines.

Tax-Deductible and Tax-Deferred Account Options

1. **401(k) and 403(b) Accounts**

Annual Contribution Limits: One hundred percent of compensation (i.e., if you make $10K, you can contribute $10K, up to $17,500 ($23,000 for those aged fifty or older).

Income Restrictions: None. This may be limited for "highly compensated employees," so check with your plan's "summary plan description" for specifics.

Investment Choice/Control: This is the only flaw to most 401(k) and 403(b) plans. Many of these plans are very limited in their investment choice. They commonly offer around twenty options, often comprised of stock, bond, and target date retirement funds (outlined in chapter five: The 401k Handcuff).

Notes: If your employer provides a matching contribution, this is probably the best investment decision you can make. Your contribution is tax deductible and the money grows tax deferred, but your employer contributes to your account by matching the contribution. For example, if the employer matches 3 percent, this means that if the employee contributes 3 percent, he or she gets a 100 percent return (via the employer contribution) in his or her retirement account. That cannot be beat.

2. **Traditional IRA**

Annual Contribution Limits: One hundred percent of compensation up to $5,500, or $6,500 for those aged fifty and older.

Income Restrictions (for deductibility of contributions): $59,000 phased out through $69,000 for single filers and $95,000 phased out through $115,000 for those who are married and filing jointly, for those who also have a retirement plan at work. $178,000 phased out through $188,000 for married couples filing jointly where the spouse who makes the IRA contribution is not covered by a workplace retirement plan and is married to someone who is covered. There is no income limit when neither spouse has a retirement plan at work.

Investment Choice/Control: Unlimited

Notes: Money can be allocated to traditional IRAs either through contributions or rollovers from other tax-deductible retirement plans. Tax deductibility on contributions might be limited due to contribution limits or income phaseouts if other tax-deductible plans are available to you, such as 401(k)s, 403(b)s. They will also be limited if you have already funded a Roth IRA (cannot fully fund both). Traditional IRAs typically play an important role in one's retirement plan. Since many are funded from a rolled-over 401(k) or 403(b) plan (which employees have funded for many years), they often represent a retiree's largest investment account as he or she enters retirement.

If your income is above the limits for obtaining a tax deduction to these accounts, nondeductible contributions are still available. This will still allow the investor to take advantage of tax-deferred growth, but there is no upfront tax deduction, and gains will be taxed as income upon withdrawal.

Tax-Deductible and Tax-Deferred Account Options for Business Owners

1. SEP IRA

Annual Contribution Limits: These can vary each year between 0 percent and 25 percent of compensation. The maximum contribution was $52,000 for 2014. Each eligible employee must receive the same percentage from the sponsor of the plan.

More specific information about the plan and a contribution calculator can be found here: www.fidelity.com/retirement-ira/small-business/sep-ira

Income Restrictions: There are no income restrictions.

Investment Choice/Control: This is unlimited, unless your specific plan restricts it.

Notes: SEP IRAs are a valuable tool for small business owners. However, if you are a one-person business, it may be more advantageous for you to open a solo 401(k) instead.

2. **Simple IRA**

Annual Contribution Limits: Up to 100 percent of compensation, with a maximum of $12,000 for 2014, or $14,500 if you are aged fifty or older.

Income Restrictions: There are no restrictions.

Investment Choice/Control: This is unlimited, unless your specific plan restricts it.

More specific information about this plan can be found here: https://www.fidelity.com/retirement-ira/small-business/simple-ira/overview

Notes: This is available for businesses with one hundred or fewer employees. Plan sponsors must provide a matching contribution to employees of 2 percent to 3 percent. Small businesses that have too many employees to make a SEP IRA financially feasible typically implement a Simple IRA. Moreover, they usually have too few employees to consider the additional costs of setting up a formal 401(k) plan.

3. **Solo (Individual or Single) 401(k)**

Annual Contribution Limits: One hundred percent of compensation up to $17,500, or $23,000 for those aged fifty or older. In addition, the business can make a tax-deductible profit-sharing contribution. The total amount of combined contributions cannot exceed $52,000 for 2014, or $57,500 for those aged fifty or older. Additional information and a contribution calculator can be found here: https://www.fidelity.com/retirement-ira/small-business/self-employed-401k/overview

Income Restrictions: There are no restrictions.

Investment Choice/Control: This is unlimited.

Notes: This is designed for business owners who do not have any full-time employees other than their spouses. Depending on one's income, this plan option may allow for more tax-deduction contributions than a SEP IRA. The salary deferral option (employee contribution) can be utilized in addition to the profit-sharing option (from the business).

Below is a sample calculator output. It shows an example of which plan a hypothetical business could contribute the most to. Notice how in this proposed scenario the solo 401(k) allows for almost twice as many contributions as the SEP IRA:

Type of business:	Sole proprietor
Age of business owner:	45
Business profit:	$100,000
Tax year:	2013
Maximum profit-sharing contribution:	$18,588
Maximum 401(k) contribution:	$17,500
Maximum solo 401(k) contribution:	**$36,088**
Maximum SEP contribution:	**$18,588**

You can run a similar calculation by visiting Fidelity's "Self-Employed Contribution Calculator" found here: https://www.fidelity.com/retirement-ira/small-business/self-employed-401k/overview

4. Defined Benefit Plans

Annual Contribution Limits: The maximum annual contribution that you can make to a defined benefit plan would be the lesser of $210,000 for 2014 or 100 percent of the participant's average compensation for the three highest consecutive years. Big picture take-away, think about six-figure annual tax-deductible contributions.

Income Restrictions: There are no restrictions.

Investment Choice/Control: This is unlimited.

Notes: This works best for businesses with consistent income and few employees, as contributions may be required on their behalf. Moreover, this works well for business owners nearing retirement age who are looking to aggressively fund a tax-deductible retirement account. For these plans to work, consistent and large annual contributions need to be made on a regular basis for a number of years. If you do not follow protocol completely, these programs may trigger undesired complications.

Putting it all together, a small business owner with a healthy cash flow could theoretically contribute to a solo 401(k) and a defined benefit plan. This combination provides the business owner with the ability to save over $260,000 into tax deductible accounts, providing huge tax savings and quickly padding their nest egg for retirement.

Tax-Deferred and Tax-Free Account Options

1. Roth IRA

Annual Contribution Limits: One hundred percent of compensation up to $5,500, or $6,500 for those aged fifty and older.

Income Restrictions: Your ability to contribute is completely phased out at $129,000 for single filers and $191,000 for those married filing jointly.

Investment Choice/Control: This is unlimited.

Notes: Outside of college accounts, Roth IRAs are one of the few tax-free vehicles that are available to most investors. Again, unlike traditional IRAs, which provide tax deductions up front but are taxed upon withdrawal, Roth IRAs work in the opposite fashion. Contributions are not tax deductible, but they do provide tax-deferred growth and tax-free withdrawals in retirement. Assuming the investor has reached age 59.5 and the account has been open for five years, withdrawals are all tax free later on. Roth IRAs not only offer total investment control, they also offer tax control. Imagine being retired and having a tax-free bucket to withdraw money from. This can reduce your overall taxable income and potentially keep you in a lower tax bracket. After contributing to your 401(k) (at least up to the level that your employer will match), it is hard to find very many flaws in the argument that a Roth IRA should be the next vehicle that you consider.

There are four interesting caveats to Roth IRAs that you should be aware of:

1. There are two categories of money that make up the Roth IRA. One is principal (money contributed) and the other is growth. Many investors are unaware of the liquidity feature of the principal. Because you have contributed after-tax money, you can withdraw that portion of the account tax free and penalty free at any time. On the other hand, you can only withdraw the growth tax free and penalty free as long as the account has been in existence for five years and the owner has surpassed the age of 59.5. This liquidity feature, which should be an option of last resort,

is useful if you need money before you reach retirement age. As we all know, life happens.
2. When investors reach the age of 70.5, they are then required to begin taking required minimum distributions from their traditional IRAs. This is not required with Roth IRA accounts.
3. Along with all of the other tax-deferred retirement plans that we have mentioned, Roth IRAs are not assessable for college financial aid. However, the Roth plan still provides some liquidity (return of principal). Therefore, this vehicle is an excellent choice if you are trying to save money for college and retirement at the same time. It should be worth noting that any withdrawal from a retirement account will be viewed as income (by financial aid formulas) in the year after you apply for financial aid, which will hurt your chances of receiving this aid in the subsequent year. Therefore, if you are awarded need-based aid, it is best to access these funds after you have filed the last financial aid form. This occurs early in the second semester of the student's junior year of college.
4. If an investor makes too much money to contribute to a Roth IRA, there may be a backdoor way to fund these accounts. *As long as the investor does not have any traditional IRAs at the time*—otherwise the strategy becomes a logistical nightmare—he or she can contribute to a nondeductible IRA, as we mentioned in the traditional IRA section. Since the income cap on Roth conversions was lifted in 2010, investors can now contribute to a nondeductible IRA and then immediately perform a Roth conversion and therefore fund the Roth IRA account.

During a Roth conversion, all money coming from an IRA that has not been taxed will be taxed, as it then enters the Roth after tax. However, a nondeductible IRA doesn't possess any untaxed portions if it has no time to grow. Therefore, as long as you do the conversion quickly, you will have no taxes to pay on the conversion.

2. Roth 401(k)

Annual Contribution Limits: One hundred percent of compensation up to $17,500 ($23,000 for those aged fifty or older)

Income Restrictions: None

Investment Choice/Control: Same as traditional 401(k)s.

Notes: You cannot fully fund both traditional and Roth IRAs in one year, and the same is true with the Roth 401(k) contribution option (in conjunction with the traditional 401(k)). The decision of which type to fund comes down to whether you want tax deductions now or tax-free withdrawals later. The math would tell us that if you think you will be in a higher tax bracket in retirement, consider the Roth 401(k). Conversely, if you will be in a lower bracket, which often is the case, take the tax deductions now. If you are going to be in the same tax bracket when you retire, there is little difference in net dollars to you.

One difference between the Roth IRA and the Roth 401(k) is that the Roth 401(k) has to abide by the 401(k) distribution rules. There is not the same liquidity feature (return of principal) that is available with the Roth IRA. In addition, a company will match contributions on a pretax basis, and this money will therefore be taxable upon distribution, even if you elect to contribute to the Roth 401(k) instead of the traditional 401(k).

Tax-Deferred and Tax-Free College Account Options

1. 529 College Savings Plan

Annual Contribution Limits: The annual gift exclusion is $14,000, or $70,000, if a five-year election is made. Section 529 plans offer a special gifting feature. Specifically, you can make a lump-sum contribution to a 529 plan of up to $70,000, elect to spread the gift evenly over five years, and completely avoid federal gift tax, provided no other gifts are made to the same beneficiary during the five-year period. A married couple can gift up to $140,000.

Income Restrictions: None

Investment Choice/Control: There are approximately ten to fifteen different options. Account holders are only allowed one investment change per year.

Notes: 529 college savings plans are the most popular college savings vehicle. Almost every state offers at least one plan option for investors to choose from. Many states have multiple choices. At the same time, these plans also happen to be the most restrictive tax-advantaged savings plans in terms of making investment choices and having control of all the accounts. Because of this, you might think that I wouldn't recommend these accounts. Now, you may not want 100 percent of your college savings to be in one account, but I do recommend that every family consider opening one. 529 plans have replaced EE savings bonds as the ideal way to give money to a friend or a family member for future college expenses. A parent can open a 529 plan and help everyone who might consider giving the student money become aware that a plan exists for the student. Plans offer deposit slips that are like coupons in a coupon book. These allow anyone to contribute to any other person's 529. For that reason alone, I recommend that every family open what I call a family 529 plan for that student. Since the student will have a college savings account, contributors can be reasonably assured that the money that they donate will be put to that specific cause and won't be spent frivolously.

Money inside these plans grows tax deferred. If the student withdraws the money for qualified college expenses, then all of the proceeds that he or she withdraws will be tax free. However, if the student receives lots of financial aid or decides not to go to college, the student will not incur a lot of qualified education expenses (which the 529 funds are designed to be allocated to). Therefore, these accounts can become overfunded, and as a result, the gains will be taxable and assessed a 10 percent penalty.

With a plethora of plans available, which one should you choose? The first place to consider is your home state. A little over half the states offer a state tax deduction. If your home state does this, then you should give that plan serious consideration. If you live in Arizona, Kansas, Maine, Missouri, or Pennsylvania, these states allow a state tax deduction (a tax parity deduction), no matter which 529 program you invest in. If your state does not offer any tax break (California, Delaware, Hawaii, Kentucky, Massachusetts, Minnesota, New Hampshire, New Jersey, and Tennessee) or does not have state income taxes (Alaska, Florida, Nevada, South Dakota, Texas, Washington, and Wyoming), then any plan from any state is worth consideration.

A list of states that offer such a tax break can be found here: http://www.finaid.org/savings/state529deductions.phtml.

Since I have a newborn and I live in Massachusetts, which does not offer a state tax deduction, I examined every plan, eventually settling on New York's Direct 529 plan (https://www.nysaves.com/content/home.html). Half of the plans offer similar or nearly identical investment options. There are few investment options and I cannot actively manage them because investors are only allowed one investment change per year. Therefore, I decided to go with one of the least expensive programs available (going back to chapter three, if I cannot be tactical, I might as well go cheap). An added benefit is that Upromise runs New York's plan. This is a free, cash-back bonus program. At the end of the day, it won't pay for college, but every dollar counts.

In conclusion, 529 savings plans are restrictive in terms of investment management. However, they are very flexible in terms of contributions, and they are very tax friendly.

2. **Coverdell Education Savings Account**

Annual Contribution Limits: $2,000 per beneficiary.

Income Restrictions: Ability to contribute is completely phased out at $110,000 for single filers and $220,000 for those married filing jointly.

Investment Choice/Control: Unlimited

Notes: Coverdell accounts offer the reverse attributes of the 529 plan. Investment choice and control is great, but contribution flexibility is extremely limited. In fact, the rules state that no more than $2,000 can be contributed on behalf of the beneficiary. If you opened a Coverdell and contributed $2,000 and Grandpa did the same without you knowing, then unfortunately penalties may be involved. It is a well-designed plan that can even be used for private high school expenses, but due to its restrictive contribution amounts, the effectiveness of this savings account is diminished.

*For additional college planning insights, consider purchasing Tim's book *Pay for College Without Sacrificing Your Retirement*.

Tax-Deferred Variable Annuity

(Not tax deductible or tax free)

Annual Contribution Limits: Unlimited (check with issuer)

Income Restrictions: None

Investment Choice/Control: Investment choice will be limited to offerings chosen by the issuer, investor has full control.

Notes: Variable annuities provide investors with tax-deferred growth. If money is withdrawn from the account, all gains will be taxed as income (as opposed to long-term capital gains), and if withdrawn before age 59.5, the gains will be subject to an additional 10 percent penalty. From a tax standpoint, these vehicles are very similar to nondeductible IRAs.

Variable annuities as a tax-deferred investment vehicle get dismissed by the majority of financial media because many contracts do carry high internal costs and large surrender charges. In addition, the argument against utilizing a variable annuity is that all gains (not principal) in the future will be taxed as income, not at the lower long-term capital gains rate. These are all valid arguments, and to provide this as broad-spectrum advice to the general public, in my view, is reasonable if you are assuming conventional wisdom investment advice.

For readers of this book, that may be a big "if"! Conventional wisdom is that you plan to buy and hold (for at least one year) each investment you choose. Again, this is conventional money management wisdom. This book, on the other hand, introduces and makes the case for less rigid strategies. Unfortunately, one of the caveats to tactical management and ongoing trading is that they produce short-term capital gains. Because of this fact, tax-deferred accounts become incredibly valuable to unconventional account managers.

Moreover, when it comes to tax-deferred variable annuities, if the right contracts are chosen, these vehicles may be very appropriate for your needs. For example, there are numerous companies with contracts that possess lower than average internal expenses that don't carry surrender charges.

In addition, if these investments are intended for retirement (post-59.5) the argument against their tax inefficiency is somewhat softened, especially in states with high tax rates (as you will see).

Tim's state of Massachusetts taxes all income at 5.25 percent except for short-term capital gains, which is taxed at 12 percent.

Therefore, if a family wanted to implement tactical strategies, be tax efficient, and would be willing to wait until age 59.5 to access the account, the tax differences may reflect the hypothetical scenario below:

A couple who are married filing jointly, living in Massachusetts, and currently in the 33 percent income tax bracket, read this book and want to utilize tactical management strategies for additional retirement dollars they have saved.

If they were to utilize tactical management (incurring short-term capital gains) in a taxable brokerage account, their tax rates would be:

    Fed: 33%   **State: 12%**   **Total: 45%**

Utilizing buy-and-hold in a taxable brokerage account:

    Fed: 15%   **State: 5.25%**   **Total: 20.25%**

Ignoring investment strategy returns, there is an obvious tax advantage to long-term investing.

However, a tax-deferred variable annuity is a retirement account. In retirement, the family's income tends to be lower along with their tax bracket. In addition, at least for the state of Massachusetts, receiving investment income as opposed to short-term capital gains is a benefit (5.25% versus 12%). If they were to take a withdrawal from the tax-deferred annuity in retirement, now being in a lower federal tax bracket, their rates may look something similar to this:

Fed: 25%   State: 5.25%   Total: 30.25%

It is still slightly higher than the taxes on a buy-and-hold strategy, but much lower than utilizing tactical strategies within a taxable account. By now, you have concluded one way or another the direction you would like to go with your portfolio management and the potential returns that can be generated. A tax-deferred variable annuity is one additional tax-efficient vehicle that can play a role in implementing proactive tactical allocation and/or trend strategies.

*Notes: Tim's state of Massachusetts does carry one of the highest taxes on short-term capital gains. For states with lower or no tax, these calculations would be less differentiating. On the flip side, for families earning over $250K there is an additional 3.8 percent tax on long-term capital gains that was not assumed. In addition, most taxable investments generate additional income (interest and dividends) along with capital gains; this was not factored in. Therefore, depending on how analytical you want to get, more variables could be factored into this hypothetical.

The big picture take-away for all the tax-deferred vehicles mentioned in this chapter is that when it comes to the strategies outlined in this book, tax-deferred vehicles dramatically improve their efficiency.

In Summary:
- **Utilizing tax-efficient accounts creates faster net worth appreciation!**

The avoidance of taxes is the only intellectual pursuit that still carries any reward.

—John Maynard Keynes

In Closing

Portfolio Moneyball

The book and film *Moneyball* is a great example of how thinking outside the box can help you accomplish goals more efficiently. It truly was a revolutionary story because its main character, Oakland A's General Manager Billy Beane, was an unconventional thinker who forever changed the management of baseball organizations. The basic premise of the story was that Beane had the challenge of putting a competitive baseball team on the field with a budget that was a fraction of some of the wealthier franchises. For the A's to be successful, the team needed to find a way to win games with lower-salaried players.

Beane and his team began to ask bigger (albeit simplistic) questions. The brainstorming went something along these lines:

Q: How do teams win games?
A: By scoring more runs than their opponents.
Q: How do you score runs?
A: By getting players on base.
Q: How do you get on base?
A: You get a hit or walk (excluding hit batters).
Q: Okay. So we need to have players get on base more often. However, with their limited budget, how much would it cost to sign players who have a high batting average?
A: Batting average is one of the most heralded statistics in baseball. The cost would be millions.

Q: How much would it cost to sign a player who statistically gets on base a lot but does so because he walks a lot and may not have a high batting average?

A: The cost would be dramatically less.

The old belief in baseball was that batting average was one of the most important statistics in baseball. The new belief is that a player's on-base percentage may be equally as valuable. This includes walks in addition to hits.

Beane focused on players who were less expensive and had high on-base percentages. He did not rely on expensive players with high batting averages. As a result, the Oakland A's had a stretch of years where they were able to consistently make the playoffs with a budget that was a fraction of the budgets of the other playoff teams. By implementing unconventional thinking, they were able to more efficiently manage their finances to achieve a high level of success.

Whether it is Billy Beane with his baseball team or you with your portfolio, the question is: Can I accomplish my objective in a more efficient manner? Often asking that one question alone will lead you to surprising personal insights that you normally wouldn't have thought of. That is the nature of unconventional, out-of-the-box thinking. Conversely, if you don't ask these questions, you will most likely be following the herd. That isn't always the worst scenario, but it is sure to be someone else's answer to a less personal goal.

Hopefully the first five chapters introduced you to some reasons why it is important to go against conventional wisdom. Most investors follow their emotions when investing. As we have seen, this produces poor results. Most investors hold false assumptions about the motivations and roles that their mutual fund managers possess and play within their portfolios. Lastly, most investors are blissfully ignorant when it comes to current debt, deficit, QE, inflation, and rising rate risks to our economic future.

Moreover, we discussed how Wall Street and conventional wisdom fail to deliver what many investors want:

1. Less volatility.
2. More downside protection. The ability to play defense and offense in their portfolio.
3. More hands-on approaches like tactical management and self-directed investments, less "do nothing" advice.

In the next six chapters, we explored various out-of-the box solutions for your consideration. Having explored all of these options in detail, you may have come to one of three conclusions.

Conclusion 1: I appreciate the information throughout the book, but I am going to continue to use my current investments and make tweaks to my portfolio when my gut tells me to do so.

Our Take: Essentially, you have chosen the path of winging it. Statistics (e.g., Dalbar's analysis) show that the odds are against you. Having said that, we wish you luck.

Conclusion 2: I found the first five chapters interesting, but the solution chapters didn't convince me to abandon buying and holding my balanced stock and bond portfolio.

Our Take: Your strategy is better than winging it—if you can stay disciplined and you do not sell your portfolio when the next major bear market hits in both stock and bond markets. Perhaps you can be a little more efficient with your buy-and-hold strategy by using low-cost index or ETF options. Companies like Vanguard and iShares even have prepackaged buy-and-hold allocation portfolios that are made up of low-cost indexes and ETFs.

Conclusion 3: I am an out-of-the-box thinker and will consider one or many of the strategies outlined in the recommendation chapters.

Our Take: I feel for you. Again, it is not easy to be an unconventional thinker and strategist. You will not be doing what your friends, families, and coworkers are doing. However, if you are at ease with that and are willing to put in extra time and effort and assume personal responsibility, then we believe that you will not only enjoy a smoother ride with less turbulence but may also achieve higher returns over time.

We wish you all the success you deserve!

Tim Higgins and Mike Hajek

www.unconventional-investing.com

CPSIA information can be obtained
at www.ICGtesting.com
Printed in the USA
FSOW04n2101030817
37220FS